JAN 0 5

DATE DUE

SEP 01 '05			
NOV 1 0 2004			
GAYLORD			PRINTED IN U.S.A.

Calm
amid
CHAOS

An Executive Guide
To Reducing Stress Through Meditation

Executive Calm Media Group
A Division of Serenity Hill Press, Inc.

CHARLES
GRAYBAR

ISBN: 0-9740265-6-5

First Edition, First Printing

Published by: Executive Calm Media Group,
a division of Serenity Hill Press, Inc.
P.O. Box 8130
Rolling Meadows, IL 60008

Executive Calm Media Group
P.O. Box 8130
Rolling Meadows, IL 60008

E-mail: info@calmamidchaos.com
Web site: www.calmamidchaos.com

Cover design: Weblinx, Inc.
Book design & production: Weblinx, Inc.

Contents

Acknowledgements

I now realize just how genuinely humble the people making those speeches at award shows really are. We've all watched how consistently every recipient follows nearly the identical script of thanking the agents, producers, directors, the cameraman's second cousin and seemingly anyone else that they might have met in the street. Until I wrote my first book and learned firsthand how many people it takes to facilitate such an effort coming to life I never understood what all the carrying on from those people was about.

As I put the finishing touches on this, my second book, I have come to fully realize that it is in the truest sense of the word, *impossible* to accomplish writing a book and living the life of an author and public speaker without an army of incredibly dedicated and selfless people along side of you. All of whom make the truly crucial elements come together like a symphony.

It is my honor to have an ever-growing chorus of key supporters. No words can ever really express the gratitude they all deserve. It is in that spirit then that any benefits readers garner from this book are dedicated to those who made this book's existence a reality. In this case, not the least of which is my editor on this project, Bruce Wexler, who has served the role of keeping a firm hand on the rudder and even pitching in now and then to pull up the sails when needed. When the wind died down and oars were required, you picked them up on your own. No more can be asked. For Patti Clements who added cogency through caution in reviewing every word, comma and more to make the work complete.

For Andy Clements who never waivers and as nearly as we can tell, never sleeps. For Catharine and David Chiesa whose wisdom is the very ground that allows my anchor to take hold and thereby to define safe waters. Susan Wisehart and Barbara Grace – two pillars of support that both inspire and guide with the gentle kindness and patience of saints. For Don & Sue Briesch who know All About Angels earthbound and otherwise.

For Jojo. No man should ever be without a compass. No person should ever have to doubt that they are loved. In you I have both. Given the challenge to cross the Universe of time and space, I would always find you.

In memory of Buddy the Bear and Windancer's Chance, whose spirits never falter, whose souls will forever inspire me and whose presence never leaves me. For Jennifer Joyful-Sundancer, whos courage is the fuel that supports my very soul.

A note from the author on the realities of executive balance

Readers should be aware that at various times in my career I have been a CEO, a corporate officer in a Fortune 100 company and held positions on several boards of directors. Having held such responsibilities, I fully recognize that it is not always possible to be as gentle and compassionate as we might hope. In the real world, sometimes we have no alternative other than to put our foot down somewhat firmly in order to get things done. If you intend to read this book you're entitled to know that the author has that reality firmly in grasp.

But the greater reality is that getting things done while continually applying the whip instead of the carrot not only desensitizes people, but it serves as a negative motivation and can have an adverse effect on efficiency and compromise loyalty over time. As significantly in my experience as a senior executive and someone that now spends the preponderance of my time in the boardroom teaching stress reduction techniques and meditation, the very process of always having to take the hard line takes its toll on us, the executives and managers as much as those that are on the receiving end of our decisions.

My experience with this particular reality came about at age 48 when in April, 2002, despite having a lifelong history of very *low* cholesterol, I opted to have a fairly routine heart scan. As it happened, the stress I'd been accumulating over the years had taken a far greater toll on my body than I ever anticipated. The test showed that my main artery was 100% blocked in 9 places and the other four arteries were 80% to 90% blocked. Even the doctors said that I should have been dead. According to the surgeon that performed the quintuple bypass a week later, I *would have* been dead within a matter of weeks, at most months had I not acted upon a vague inclination to have the test.

What I've learned most is that in our executive job description of being always tough, resilient and always appearing unfazed by whatever daunting tasks we have to take on, the immutable underlying reality is that the stress is there whether we want to admit it, acknowledge it or deal with it. We are not defenseless though. By far the best approach that will serve your interests, your company's, your family's and the people with whom you work is one where you either get rid of the stress as soon as possible after you take it on or better yet, to never take the stress load on in the first place. A balanced approach will always yield greater results and, as importantly, increase your own inner peace and at the same time, interestingly enough, make you a far more effective executive.

This book is about the dealing with the reality of the executive stress challenge then; balancing the inordinate responsibilities of your job against your explicit responsibility to not allow it to kill you. Remember, none of what you earn means much if you don't come home in once piece to share it with those whom you love.

Introduction

I distinctly recollect the day when I first recognized that I was so overwhelmed with the sheer volume and speed at which the world was coming at me that I didn't think that I could make it another minute. Much less another day.

Like everyone else, I had a boss, a spouse, family obligations, community obligations, lawyers, accountants – a seemingly endless stream of people and situations all pulling mercilessly on me from every direction. Everyone needed an answer now. Right now.

When that day came to an end, I lay in bed trying everything I could to slow down enough to get a few hours sleep. I knew that I would have to get up and do the same thing all over again the next day and the day after that. As I lay there trying to unwind, my empathy with those poor people down at the Post Office increased as I could feel what it was like to have the onslaught of things coming at you never stop. Or slow down. Ever.

I definitely had the feeling that something major was missing from my life. Fortunately, I found a way to change my trajectory.

1

Since you've made it to the point where you've picked up this book, chances are that you recognize that there's something essentially absent from your life in much the same way as I did back then. Some like to think of it as just basic peace and quiet. Others seek a deeper feeling – the achievement of a true state of inner calm. But no matter what we might call it, what we all crave in this non-stop, cockamamie world is shelter – even just a brief respite — from the emotional, psychological and physiological assaults that we all endure merely by living our lives in the world as it is today.

That such a state of calm and inner quiet is so universally and desperately desired is evidenced by the behaviors we resort to in our efforts to fend off the world from intruding into our peace of mind. Alcoholism has left no executive suite or family untouched. The so-called "mood-leveling prescription compounds" that range from Prozac to Valium are doled out to the hyper-stressed executives, stay-at home moms and dads and even children that are under constant psychological assault merely by virtue of the daily state of their existence. Such solutions to our challenges in dealing with the world are, at best, mere band-aids applied over our gaping and festering wounds.

Back in the mid-1980s I found myself in exactly this state of mind — what I retrospectively call "true executive distress." The company I was running had encountered some very rough waters and there were significant underlying dynamics occurring in the market we operated in that made escape from our dilemma seem all but impossible. Like everyone else that encounters deep levels of stress at work, those problems bled over into my personal life. My day-to-day existence had turned into a living nightmare. The anxiety and stress were starting to take a toll on me and I knew I couldn't possibly fend it all off indefinitely.

Over the years a number of friends and associates had suggested to me that I explore meditation as a mechanism to help me counteract the stress in my life. I would usually respond with something like, "Who has time to run off to India and sit on top of a mountain with a guru?" Or more often, "Who has time for such a thing period?" Today, when I suggest to others that they meditate, I usually get, "I could never concentrate well enough to do something like that."

Executive friends of mine who have struggled with alcohol over the years have told me that in order for them to finally reach out and accept help with their problem, they had to get to a point of real suffering, a point almost beyond pain. Now, of course, I can empathize with them because as the crises in my own career were worsening, I found that I was willing to try anything short of alcohol or pharmaceuticals to alleviate the stress and overall dissatisfaction with life that I was suffering through every day.

As it turns out, this story has a happy ending. Despite years of telling people that I could never learn to meditate, that I didn't have time for it and all the other excuses I manufactured back then, I did learn to meditate. For me, it was simply a matter of survival, a defining moment when I was forced to choose between a life that was barely tolerable and a life of growth in every meaningful way imaginable. I chose the latter.

Experiencing peace of mind, learning to find true balance in all of my relationships, experiencing tremendous spiritual growth and, oddly enough, increasing my income were all products of my learning the most basic skills of meditation. As I enhanced my knowledge and practice in meditation, I significantly extended the depth of those benefits.

Many people have asked me if my present state of contentment is really attributable to the meditation. The answer is always a resounding, yes! The fact is, meditation is no more and no less than a way for us to make a connection of higher integrity with our truest selves. It is almost as though the cable connected to the back of our television sets isn't completely in the socket and because of that, the signal gets obscured with a lot of interference. Meditation is a method for clearing the debris out of the pathway between our deepest "mind" and our ability to apply that mind to the challenges we face in our everyday world. It teaches us to meet those challenges with true equanimity.

Now, it is true that the pursuit of meditation to the deepest levels through some of the more advanced practices can open our eyes and our souls to unimaginable spiritual insights and levels of unprecedented inner calm. Such levels of insight hold the promise of revealing the secrets of our true natures. But for the average person seeking greater levels of satisfaction and happiness in their lives and tools to enhance their resilience against the onslaught of the world, great benefits can be derived from the more basic practices. And a time commitment of not much more than 30 minutes a day is all that is required.

Along with the minimal time commitments, there is another prerequisite to getting to the place where your efforts in meditation will bring about the changes you seek: determination. One cannot succeed in deriving the benefits of meditation without the determination to consistently execute the practices. You will need to have faith that the benefits lag behind the effort to some degree.

At first, these benefits may be subtle. But the pay off from your efforts will be worth it. Ask yourself this: if it were a matter of money, what would you pay to find the calm amid the chaos in your daily life? What would it be worth to you to begin and end each day with a sense of balance and a feeling of peace in your mind? Without having to think about it for a long time I've had many people answer that with a resounding, "Anything! Everything!"

I do have one major piece of advice to those attempting to learn meditation from this book or through any other source. If you find yourself getting frustrated at any point, loosen your grip; it means you're trying too hard. Meditation requires some patience in order to arrive at the place where benefits accrue.

4

As I state in Chapter 10, the end of this book is the beginning of the process. Only by applying what you have learned for 10 or 15 minutes twice a day, every day, will the miracle of meditation bring about the peace and other benefits so many – including professionals in the traditional medical community — are speaking about.

If you experience any difficulties as you go through the exercises, refer to the troubleshooting section at the end of each chapter. Do not, under any circumstances, move on to the next chapter unless you have completed the exercise outlined in the current one. If it takes you a few extra days to complete the course, take it. Failure to do so would be like laying bricks on top of a preceding layer without allowing the mortar to set. You know what will happen.

Just remember, meditation – taking the mind to a place of sustained calmness and quiet – is actually our natural state. It is the constant noise of the world and the pressure created by our daily endeavors that create all of the disturbances that we seek to overcome. By applying meditation as a technique to reacquaint the mind with the concept of quiet, we can start to shield ourselves from this noise and pressure.

Keep to no more than one chapter per day. Do the practices as they are described. Have patience. It took a long time to get your mind this cluttered and distracted. It may take a while to clear your mind and reach a state of deep inner calm, happiness and peace.

You will get there. Just do the work.

Chapter One

— Problem Recognition —

I am a firm believer in asking for assistance when I need it. Back in the mid-1980s, when I was a busy COO, I never hesitated engaging a consultant when my company needed a solid push in the right direction. So when I wanted to learn to meditate and had some serious difficulty getting started, I chose to deal with this challenge in a similar way.

Through an odd series of events, I came to meet an aging Buddhist monk named Dzongsar. After several visits to the old monk, during which we discussed the difficulties I was experiencing in my attempts at meditation, I finally managed to convey to him my fears that I might actually be incapable of learning how to meditate. After all, even though I certainly had a strong desire to meditate, I'd already failed in several attempts to go it on my own. On about my seventh visit, Dzongsar said to me, "Learning to meditate would not be so difficult if one didn't need to exist in the world at the same time."

As I began to object to the ambiguity of his comment, Dzongsar held up one finger and smiled. He'd done this on previous occasions, and I'd learned that he wanted me to find the lesson in what he had already said. I knew that he expected me to take some time to think about his comments before returning for further instruction.

Being involved in business at the executive level while simultaneously being asked to ponder complex Buddhist philosophical mysteries was about as contrary a set of challenges as I could imagine facing. Yet the more I thought about what the old Buddhist monk had said to me, the more determined I became to solve the puzzling nature of his comment. Doing so while being distracted by my usual jousting with investment bankers and the other knights of the business realm wasn't a particularly easy task. I recognized how distracted and unfocused I'd actually become because of my work.

That should have been my first clue.

Unable to penetrate the mystery within the koan[1] the monk had presented me with, I nevertheless went back to see him about two weeks later. After making my offering of fresh fruit to the monastery, as was my usual custom upon first arriving, Dzongsar smiled, motioned for me to sit down in front of him, and with a subtle motion of his head, invited me to proceed with my questions.

I nodded, cleared my throat and just as I was about to begin objecting that the lesson the old monk had given me was too vague, he quickly reached over and picked up a short stick with padding on the end – the kind you'd use for beating a kettle drum – and struck a large brass gong that was directly

---

[1] *Koan /koh' an/ n.*
(1) A puzzling, often paradoxical statement or story used in Zen Buddhism as an aid to meditation and as a means of gaining spiritual awakening. (2) A Zen teaching riddle, most commonly identified with Renzei Zen Buddhism. Koans are attractive paradoxes to be meditated on; their purpose is to help one to enlightenment by temporarily jamming normal cognitive processing so that something more interesting can happen.

behind him. He hit it only once but the sound was so shattering and his movements so uncharacteristically fast that it scared the hell out of me. My attention was fixed on the sound produced by that huge metal gong.

Dzongsar sat there with great serenity. As I started to ask what he wanted to convey through his actions, he just smiled at me and said, "Follow the sound to wherever it goes." I considered that comment for a few seconds. As I began to seek clarification on this strange instruction, Dzongsar shook his head slightly and repeated, "Follow the sound to wherever it goes."

I noticed that as he repeated this, he closed his eyes and sat in what looked to be absolute peace and comfort. In fact, he looked the very picture of what one might expect to grace the cover of any book on meditation. I would have given almost anything to be able to reach such a state of inner calm.

The sound of the large gong was still reverberating loudly in the air so I decided to try to emulate the old monk's actions and comply with his mysterious directive. As I closed my eyes and concentrated solely on the sound of the gong , I was quite surprised to find that as I focused on the sound, the rest of the world seemed to melt away into a vague near nothingness. It was as if in that moment, the only thing that existed was the sound of the gong's distant echo. As its reverberation faded, I concentrated on the shards of sound that remained. The more intently I focused, the deeper the rest of the world receded into the background of my awareness.

After a while – I really couldn't tell how long it had been – I opened my eyes and saw the old monk watching me with a broad smile. I'd never seen him smile before and it evoked a genuine feeling of happiness and peace in me. Just as I was about to ask the monk a question about what had just transpired, he held up his hand to silence me. With his eyes wide and innocent like a child's he said, "Now, what was it you were asking before about wanting to learn to meditate?"

In a moment of true awakening and revelation, *I* was now

the one grinning from ear to ear. Without needing to read 30 books, go to Tibet, or learn to chant complex mantras, the old monk had demonstrated the essential, basic state we reach when we meditate. He'd distracted my mind in one swift and definitive action. He had literally *forced* my attention to focus on the sound of the gong – and only the sound of the gong.

But Dzongsar had done something else, which was the true brilliance of his incremental teaching. He'd shown me the answer to the mysterious koan. What Dzongsar had really been communicating when he presented me with the koan was that learning to meditate would be easy if it weren't for all of the distractions, including our internal chatter, caused by the challenges of engaging in our daily activities. When the old monk struck the gong, he distracted me from that chatter. Rather than indulging in incessant internal dialogue – perhaps about how I needed to get to the bank so I could get some leases refinanced and meet a key objective of my business strategy—my mind became clearly focused on just the sound of the gong. And as my focus changed, my mind's ability to quell that chatter increased.

Our minds, in their most natural – call it primordial – state, are quiet, and free of the turmoil that we have to deal with every minute of every day. From the time we are infants, our minds become cluttered with debris. We are are ceaselessly challenged to cope with all kinds of distractions.

This is especially true for business executives. Just consider all the input you receive from different mediums the moment you walk in the office: phone, fax, e-mail and old-fashioned print correspondence (memos, letters, etc.). In fact, think about how you now receive this input even when you're not in the office due to new technologies. On planes, in cars and even when you're supposedly relaxing at home on a weekend, people can and do reach you with all sorts of messages and requests. Just as significantly, your mind is cluttered with overwhelming amounts of information that makes decision-making harder rather than easier. Every minute seems to bring fresh information about markets, trends and competitors' moves that have to be processed. Not only is it difficult to process all this information, but the processing itself catalyzes all sorts of questions and decision points that further clutter the mind.

Meditation clears this debris, eliminating these distractions from our consciousness.

Dzongsar's gong had an additional effect. It forced me to focus solely on one – and *only* one – thing for those few moments. And that "thing" wasn't a thought, a problem, an idea or a conflict that was gnawing away at me. The all-consuming ring of the gong wasn't something that could distract me in any negative way, and negativity was the state of mind I lived in virtually all day long.

I enjoyed another benefit from this brief exercise. For those few minutes that my mind **wasn't** engaged in its customary roiling, anxious, conflicted self-debate, it was in an unprecedented state of rest. When we achieve a true meditative state – even for just a few moments — our active mind goes on vacation. The relief and release is reminiscent of the feeling we achieve from sitting on a beach for a few days and not doing a thing. The results are the same even though the release occurs for a very brief period of time.

Meditation removes the ring of phones and faxes, the sound our computer makes when we have e-mail, and all of the other noises in our lives that drive us to distraction. It also temporarily removes even the concept that those things exist. When it does that, our minds go into a virtual shutdown mode. The result: an incredibly relaxed, peaceful, and refreshed state. The more we meditate, the more "vacation" we give the mind, the longer and deeper these benefits extend.

The inner peace that I felt as I walked to my car outside the monastery that day was unlike anything I'd ever felt. I went back to my office and accomplished more in one afternoon than I would normally have been able to take on in several days.

More importantly, I no longer considered every person I dealt with that day to be an adversary. I felt at peace with myself and the world around me. Bear in mind, this was after one experience with meditation. One. It had lasted maybe 30 seconds.

As the monk showed me, learning to meditate isn't particularly difficult, but there is a bit of spadework that needs to be performed. To begin your journey, you'll need to follow the lesson outlined below exactly as described to get your mind to a place where you feel the effects of "following the gong."

Lesson #1: Understanding the Monkey Mind

Meditation is about quieting the mind. But before you move to an internal place where you can get to a true meditative state, it helps to understand some of the challenges you might face in getting there.

Anyone who works in the corporate environment is familiar with the most basic concept of problem solving. In order to solve any problem, you need to have a clear, concise and accurate understanding of exactly what the problem is. Here's an example of what happens when you fail to do just that.

I recently dropped my car off at a shop that had been servicing my vehicles for years. When I returned to pick it up, the always amiable owner of the shop, informed me, "O.K. Chuck, you're all set now; you've got four new radials on there, no worries now!"

Unfortunately, the tires on this car had had been replaced just a few weeks earlier. I'd left the car there to have the radiator fixed. Obviously, the radiator wasn't going to get fixed until this man had a clear and concise understanding of the problem.

Misunderstanding the precise nature of the problem is where people new to meditation often go astray. Lesson #1 will help you to understand the problem most people suffer from when they set out to learn meditation. It demonstrates the kind of noise that goes on in our minds continuously without our awareness or acknowledgement. This noise has been given many names by teachers of meditation: "monkey mind," "the internal dialogue," "the tireless voice" and a slew of others. Regardless of what you call it, becoming acquainted with your mind's chatter is the first step to embracing meditation.

Exercise #1: Observing the Monkey Mind

Meditation requires a quiet and undisturbed environment. You need to find a place with no phones, faxes, and e-mails nagging you for a response. If you need to, go outside and find a park bench or some other place where you can sit without external distraction for 15 minutes. Many executives I know escape to their cars for 10 or 15 minutes during the business day to meditate or they seek out an unused office and close the door. Stay at home moms and dads wait until nap time or trade off with other parents to secure the magical 15 minutes they need for this work.

This exercise is called "observing the monkey mind." Don't worry about doing it incorrectly. All the exercise requires is that you observe the way your mind functions. It takes five minutes at this stage and needs to be done once in the morning of your first day and once at night. Here are the exercise's steps:

♦ Get a piece of paper and something to write with.

♦ Go to wherever you will be meditating and do all that you can to make the environment peaceful and comfortable. You may sit in a chair or on the floor.

♦ Make sure you have a clock or a watch to record the time at various junctures in the exercise.

♦ Make a note of your "start time." Close your eyes and try to clear your mind completely. Do not get frustrated if you have difficulty clearing your mind. This is the entire purpose of this exercise. Just do the best you can to gently quiet your mind. This is not an internal wrestling match. The goal is to allow your mind to go wherever it wants to go.

♦ Observe and take mental note of what comes into your thoughts. This must be done without judgment or criticism. You are *not* failing at your first attempt in meditation if you have difficulty focusing your mind. Just pay attention to your thoughts. There is no such thing as a good or a bad thought.

♦ Continue to observe the thoughts and ideas and feelings that appear – no matter what they are – for what you think is about five minutes. When it seems like five minutes have passed, open your eyes.

♦ Look at the clock; write down the "end time" of your first session.

♦ Write down as many of the thoughts, ideas, feelings that entered your mind as you attempted to quiet your thoughts. Write down everything no matter how insignificant it might seem. It's your list — no one else will ever see it — so be honest about what you experienced, how much came into your mind and any challenges that you had quieting your mind. Someday very soon you'll look back at this list in amazement, so retain it.

If you are like 99.9% of the people that try meditation, this was probably a fairly frustrating experience for you. Your mind jumped from one thing to another. When one thought left – or maybe you tried to throw it out – another took its place.

Congratulations. You've now taken the first step toward understanding how your own mind actually operates. Like an attic cluttered with junk, your mind has become a storage facility for every piece of information thrown at you throughout your life. Just look at what accumulates on a typical day. You are jerked out of a sound sleep by the screech of the alarm clock. You drive to work, cell phone attached to one ear as you strain with the other to follow the traffic report on the radio. You attend drawn-out meetings and participate in never-ending conference calls. You confront problem after problem at work, only to return home to face challenges in your personal life. Is it any wonder that you feel overloaded and overwhelmed? That your first attempt to quiet your mind feels more like a replay of the day's events than a trip to nirvana?

Given all this clutter, your mind is left with no choice but to race just to keep up with the growing pile of ideas, information and issues. In a continuous self-dialogue, you banter with yourself in an effort to cope with and create solutions to all that you have tossed into your attic. Cleaning up this mess will help you enhance your functionality, improve your relationships and achieve greater peace of mind and happiness.

Troubleshooting

Do not be alarmed if you experience a fairly strong reaction to your first attempt to meditate. Strong reactions are often by-products of early attempts to quiet the mind. Our minds produce a variety of thoughts, strong emotions and moods. We all learn to control these elements to one degree or another, and sometimes this internal control mechanism lies just below consciousness. Other times, we're aware that we are consciously suppressing something – we know when we're making an effort not to lose our temper, for example.

In order to censor these strong feelings, we expend significant energy holding them inside. When we quiet the mind with meditation by relaxing some of these "control gates," uncomfortable thoughts and emotions can rise to the surface. So don't be surprised at anything you might experience. You might confront powerful feelings, recollections of past events and even traumas as you practice the earlier stages of learning meditation.

Several years ago I had agreed to teach a small group of acquaintances how to do basic meditation. They were all professionals, mid- to upper-tier executives and one physician. Since I didn't happen to have a six foot gong with me at the time, I started with a basic instruction and exercise into the "monkey mind."

As I guided the group through the initial part of the exercise and assured them that there was no way to "fail" in this effort, I noted that they all were able to relax. In no time at all the entire room quieted down as each individual began to focus his or her attention on the exercise. Never one to pass up an opportunity to meditate, I closed my eyes and slipped into the early stages of my personal preferred meditation technique – something called "the Twin Hearts Chakra meditation."

Just at the point where I would have normally gone very quiet internally, I was jolted into consciousness by one of the women in the group yelling, "Shut up…just shut the hell up!" She scared the living daylights out of the entire group and, needless to say, the teaching of meditation was over for that evening.

This woman was, of course, addressing her frustration at being unable to control her own mind. She was shocked to learn that she "spoke" to herself constantly.

I reassured her that such an experience is no different than cleaning out the attic and coming across an embarrassing letter written years ago or an old photo that conjured an unpleasant memory. I invited her to accept the object for what it was – a remnant from her past — and deal with it in any way that she chose to. Some people would want to throw it away. Others might have some sentimental attachment to it and decide to place it in a more prominent place in the house as a reminder not to make the same mistake again. It was her choice.

If, as you work through Lesson #1, you too encounter remnants from your past, feel free to dispose of them as you see fit. And continue the work. With each attempt at meditation you will find less and less debris cluttering your own mind's attic.

Chapter Two
— Mindfulness 101 —

Now that you've been introduced to the monkey mind, the next step is to begin practicing the techniques that will modulate your internal dialogue in stages. As your internal dialogue becomes fainter, you will begin reaching some of the upper levels of your mind's attic where the good stuff is stored. The technique we'll be using to reach those serene levels is called "mindfulness."

Mindfulness is both a methodology and a practice. Many noted Buddhist practitioners — the famous Lama Thich Nhat Hanh among them — have spent their entire lives immersed in the practice of mindfulness. Since this book is written primarily for those at the earlier stages of learning meditation, the practices and techniques discussed here will focus on quieting the internal dialogue. By way of full disclosure though, you should be aware that mindfulness is a truly magnificent and powerful method. If practiced diligently under a true master, mindfulness can lead to awakenings and enlightenment of the soul.

The previous chapter's exercise actually introduced you to a very early-stage experience in mindfulness. The practice of mindfulness, at least as we will be applying it in the Graybar Method, involves a heightening of our awareness by simply paying attention. Mindfulness can be applied to any thing or any function that we engage in. Driving the car. Watching our children play. Observing a bird making its nest in a tree outside our window.

The difference between what we do as we go about our daily activities and the practice of mindfulness is subtle. Mindfulness involves being completely absorbed and aware that we are *doing* the activity that we are involved in as opposed to simply going through the motions. If I asked you what you are doing right now, your answer would be that you are reading a book on meditation. If I asked you to be mindful of what you are doing right now, you would take yourself to a place of *conscious awareness* that you are reading this book. Someone practicing mindfulness would say out loud or silently acknowledge, "I am reading a book," at the same time he or she were actually engaged in this activity. Sounds like splitting hairs, doesn't it? Here's my first experience in attempting to unsplit these hairs and a taste of the frustration that I experienced in sorting all this out for the first time.

To this day, if I close my eyes I can still see Dzongsar's face as he explained mindfulness to me. His eyes were as bright as searchlights because he could see how frustrated I was at deciphering the seemingly pointlessness and supposedly subtle distinction between doing a thing and being aware that you are doing it. With each explanation offered, I became more and more frustrated. He never lost his patience. He never became frustrated.

Finally, Dzongsar seemed to sense that I was about to give up for the day. He smiled and told me that he'd *show* me the difference in a way that I'd never forget and, at the same time, teach me an essential meditation technique that I would keep for all of my future lifetimes. It sounded a bit like a used car sales pitch but, as I recalled the profound impression the gong exercise had left on me, I decided that I had little to lose and everything to gain from at least trying whatever the old monk had in mind.

Dzongsar sat quietly for several minutes. Just as I was about to ask him if I should come back at some later date, he said, "Are you breathing?" His question caught me so much by surprise that it actually took me a few moments to answer. "Well, of course I'm breathing, Dzongsar. If I wasn't, who do you think you'd be having this conversation with?"

In all of the time I spent visiting Dzongsar over the years, this was the one and only time I would ever hear him laugh out loud, albeit good-naturedly. His eyes lit up even brighter than before as he smiled and responded, "Oh, so you want to jump right into the *really* advanced lessons and skip the basic ones!" Although I didn't know it at the time, Dzongsar was referring to one of the tenants of Zen that falls under the general subject area of nihilism[2]. This particular belief suggests the possibility that nothing actually exists other than thought and, as such, no conversation is ever actually taking place between two entities that are imagining they are actually people.

Years later I was finally able to understand what Dzongsar had found so funny about my challenge that day. At the time, though, I answered the old monk that I was confident that I *was* in fact, breathing. Dzongsar replied, "Good, this exercise would have been a bit more difficult had you not been certain of that."

I'll assume for the sake of argument that if you are reading this that you too must be breathing.

---

[2]*nihilism / ni` el iz ‘em/ n.*
(1) An extreme form of skepticism that denies all existence. (2) A doctrine holding that nothing can be known or communicated; skepticism as to all knowledge and all reality. (3) Rejection of all distinctions in moral or religious value and a willingness to repudiate all previous theories of morality or religious belief.

Lesson 2: Practicing Mindfulness

Again, mindfulness is awareness of what you are doing at any moment. But as you will learn, mindfulness applied against certain exercises can serve to quiet the mind by distracting it from many of its normal monkey-like activities. This occurs very subtly at first and, as you become more proficient in the practice of mindfulness, you'll turn down your internal dialogue's volume to the point that it occurs below the level of conscious awareness. The mindfulness practices must be done without focus on the objective of quieting the mind.

Mindfulness is somewhat like using the TV remote control. It's enough to know that they "work". While it may be that some very inquisitive types might need to know specifically *how* it works, most are satisfied that it changes the channel, adjusts the volume and controls the all important mute function. In this case, it is that same "mute" button that we hope to push through the consistent practice of mindfulness.

Do not allow yourself to become distracted during this exercise. This one is different from the monkey mind exercise when you let your mind run wherever it wanted to. Mindfulness involves an early stage focusing on whatever activity is being engaged in. While advanced practitioners might effect mindfulness in some scenarios by saying something like, "Now my mind is running amuck thinking about all sort of crazy, unfocused things," early practitioners must try to remain more focused than that.

Remember, mindfulness is conscious awareness and acknowledgment of whatever we are doing, no matter what that is. As I am writing this sentence in this book, I am saying to myself, "Now I am writing a sentence in a book." Just trust that there is a reason for this and that the results will be self evident as you learn and practice.

Exercise 2: Mindfulness of Breath

You need to go to the place where you have decided to practice your mediation and take the steps required to assure a quiet, peaceful setting.

♦ Get into a comfortable position. Again, if sitting on the floor is more comfortable than in a chair, feel free to do so. What is most important here is that the position itself is not a source of distraction and that you are comfortable.

♦ Begin by thinking about the most peaceful and restful state you can recall having experienced in your life. Possibly you were on a beach on a sparsely populated island with only the waves as background sound. Perhaps there was a moment with someone you truly love where for just an instant you became fully lost in each other's eyes. Whatever the deeply-affecting event or scenario might have been, think through each detail meticulously. If you were outside, what was the sky like? What was the temperature? Use your mind to recreate the scene. What did you actually *feel* like that makes this particular experience so memorable? Recollect the way you felt then and allow yourself to *feel* that way now. If you are recalling a moment that you were loved, feel that love again at your solar plexus. Focus only on that feeling.

♦ Now, as you allow yourself to bask in that feeling, take in a slow, deliberate, deep breath. As you breathe in, imagine that you enhance your ability to relive that place – that experience – with even greater clarity. Be aware that as you breathe in, each detail of the image becomes more vivid. As you hold your breath for just a few moments, feel the image becoming even sharper, each detail exploding with crisp acuity. Now, slowly let that breath go and be aware of the fact that you are exhaling. As you exhale, *feel* yourself doing so. As you exhale, say to yourself, "Now I am exhaling."

♦ Take another slow, deliberate breath in and as you do so, become conscious that you are inhaling. Feel the air going into your lungs. As you inhale, remember that you are enhancing the feeling of a particular memory to its highest level of clarity. As you breathe in, though, be aware that you are doing so and say to yourself, "Now I am breathing in."

♦ Continue this pattern for about 10 minutes. Remember, each time you inhale, the scene you are recollecting becomes clearer. Every feeling you felt then increases as you inhale. As you inhale, remind yourself that you are doing so. "Now I am inhaling" is a primary exercise in mindfulness. "Now I am exhaling" is another primary exercise in mindfulness. The objective is to focus on the breath. You need accomplish no more in this particular exercise than to become aware that you *are* inhaling and exhaling in a normal pattern and at a very comfortable pace.

Many practitioners of meditation achieve very comfortable – sometimes near blissful —states of mind after focusing on the enhancement of the "place" or "experience." If that occurs for you, feel free to bask in this comforting place for an extended period of time.

After 10 minutes or so of this exercise, you need to take a moment to be mindful of the scene and of feeling the experience that you started out with. How has it grown? Has it become more vivid because you added clarity to it with each breath? As you became aware that the 10-minute time objective was approaching, were you genuinely mindful of each breath in and each breath out?

This is one of the most powerful, yet simplest forms of meditation practice. Becoming mindful and focusing on one's breathing is not only a key foundational exercise of meditation practice, but it also serves to shift our focus away from the distractions of our everyday world. While our focus has been moved away, even gradually, from the complex business deals, problems with bosses and other vexing issues, our minds rest.

This basic mindfulness exercise should be performed both in the mornings and evenings of the second, third, fourth and fifth days of practice. If, as a product of performing this specific exercise in mindfulness, you obtained a particular feeling of peace and relaxation, perform this exercise as often as you'd like.

Many executives who practice meditation will perform a breath mindfulness exercise about 15 minutes or so in advance of an event that they know will be stressful. I generally do so before every public address that I give, and I am completely at ease during these talks. Many times, business professionals perform below expectations because their minds aren't clear. They rehearse the conversation they're going to have with a boss or direct report so many times that it prevents them from responding to anything but the rehearsed conversation; they're not prepared to deal with unexpected turns in the discussion. Or it may be that they're so nervous or fearful about a presentation or a performance review that they let their feelings get in the way of what they want to say.

If you're like most business executives, your mind is filled with a web of thoughts and emotions. There is so much pressure on you and so many issues to deal with that you likely become caught in this web and can't give your full intellectual and emotional attention to the matter at hand. Breath mindfulness, however, can untangle the web and provide you the space you need to be relaxed and focused.

Extra Credit

For those that used to like to polish an apple and leave it on the teacher's desk at the end of class, you might find this little exercise interesting. It is done at night before you go to sleep on the second through the fifth nights.

As you prepare to go to sleep, quiet your mind in the same way that you did when you began to recollect the idyllic scene. As you begin to get that scene in your mind's eye, stop and ask yourself, "Who or what is it that is 'mindful' and who or what is saying 'Now I am breathing in, now I am breathing out?'"

Don't be surprised at anything that occurs after that. Do, however, enjoy and contemplate the potential meaning of the experience.

Troubleshooting

Some people have a bit of difficulty with expressing the obvious. In fact, when Dzongsar first instructed me in this practice and he told me to say, "Now I am inhaling," I instead uttered, "Now I am acting like a buffoon." Dzongsar reached under his mat, took out his kettledrum stick and gently bonked me on the head! With a terse smile, Dzongsar then said, "Now you are mindful of needing to get ice for your head!"

Reassure yourself that no one knows what you are saying and no one knows what you are doing when you execute this practice. Remember, certain meditative acts need to be done with faith that they work. In the Graybar Method, mindfulness practice provides the foundation upon which all subsequent meditation practices will be built.

If you're still having trouble, shorten the exercise. Some students have told me that they experience difficulty in concentrating on their breath and the image or feeling that invokes serenity at the same time. If this is the case, let go of the imagery or the feeling and begin the practice by concentrating solely on the breath. Begin with just one inhalation and one exhalation. And you needn't scream out, "Now I am breathing in! Now I am breathing out!" You are pursuing awareness, not invoking a mantra. The idea is for you to be *aware* of what you are doing and acknowledge that awareness through the process of being mindful of it to yourself.

Chapter Three
—Beginning Awareness—

In order to quiet the mind, we need to give it as few distractions as possible. The Graybar Method deals with the clutter in the attic in two ways. First, it helps you locate and clear out the clutter that you've already accumulated over the years. Second, it provides a way to avoid allowing clutter to accumulate in the first place.

If you are following the exercises in this book as presented, you have already been practicing "active mindfulness," for five days. Now let's explore a practice called "functional mindfulness."

If practiced intelligently, functional mindfulness can be an incredibly powerful tool, not only for meditation but in helping us manage our everyday lives. Think about it. Who, if they were actually "mindful" of what they were doing, would find themselves saying, "Now I'm treating my direct report like a slave by ordering him to phone a customer we both know I should be calling?" The fact is, we are not usually very mindful as we go about our daily business.

I certainly wasn't functionally mindful until I learned to meditate in the mid-80's. In fact, I was made acutely aware of this deficiency in the mid-80's when I walked into the Buddhist monastery, made my offering and tracked down Dzongsar. He was standing in his garden, clipping a flowering bush meticulously. Only later did I learn that he was actually practicing mindfulness.

As Dzongsar saw me approaching, he waved and motioned for me to sit down. Before I had a chance to say anything, he asked, "So what did you do today?" I began to summarize my activities. When I had listed all that I had accomplished through about lunchtime, Dzongsar held up his hand to stop my monologue. He peered directly at me for a moment and asked again, "No, what did you *do* today?"

It required a bit of back and forth with the old monk for me to understand what he really wanted: To slow down the pace of my "replay tape" and carefully report on some of the more subtle details of my activities.

Trying to comply, I mentioned that I had stopped at the gas station on Sepulveda and filled up my car. After Dzongsar admonished me to add a bit more detail I said, "Oh, well, I stopped by the gas station on Sepulveda to get gas. I think the kid that works there is mildly retarded. He was incredibly slow today and…oh…I think I said something I shouldn't have…." I realized then that I had been unkind and impatient with the boy who was undoubtedly doing the best that he could.

What I found most interesting about this exercise was not only how abrasive and insensitive I had been to the gas station kid, but also how unaware I had been that I was behaving in that way.

Every single thing we do – or in some cases, things that we didn't do that we know we should have – gets tossed into the mind's attic.

My behavior toward the gas station attendant was tossed into my attic. The mere fact that I could recount what I did so accurately without having taken conscious note of the time was proof that this act resided there. Where there were no immediate repercussions from my behavior, I learned that if I kept filling my attic with negativity, its contents would eventually overflow the attic's limited space and impact other aspects of my life.

By practicing mindfulness, we begin to "know" when we have done – or not done – something that we don't feel too great about. It helps us to become aware of what we're putting in our attics and (ideally) helps us keep them neat and tidy. Once we get the hang of practicing mindfulness, we can become vigilant about filling the space in our attics with undesirable clutter. That's the real reward, as the following anecdote illustrates.

Mike, a neighbor down the street, kindly agreed to host our annual neighborhood block party last year. All the men at the party ended up congregating outside our host's garage. Actually, we were standing around oohing and aahing at the cleanest garage any of us had ever seen, a true monument to orderliness and organization. We were looking at a suburban anomaly — an uncluttered garage, completely void of power tools, lawn maintenance equipment, painting supplies, and kids' bicycles.

"Holy mackerel!" one of the neighbors exclaimed, "How the heck do you do that, Mike?" Mike looked back at us and asked, "Do what?" A few of the guys responded in unison, "Keep your garage so uncluttered!" Mike looked as if we had just asked him how he managed to keep breathing all day long. He glanced back over his shoulder at his pristine garage, smiled at us and said, "Oh, it's not too hard actually, I just don't put much in there."

Had Dzongsar been at the block party, he no doubt would have bowed and placed a gold star on Mike's head. As Mike had so succinctly pointed out, one of the most effective ways to reduce clutter is to simply avoid accumulating too much stuff. Through mindfulness, we can create a self-styled sentry of sorts

31

that sounds the alarm at the sight of anyone or anything approaching that has the potential to create more clutter.

Functional mindfulness helps us to eliminate – or at least reduce the number of – obstacles and trash we place in our minds. It is a sentry of awareness if you will.

Lesson 3: Practicing Functional Mindfulness

In western cultures in particular, the purpose of practicing functional mindfulness is to spotlight certain thoughts, actions and intentions that arise daily. By becoming aware of theose parts of ourselves, we may decide that we'd be better off without some of them or we may choose to at least modify them.

If you think back to the "monkey mind" exercise, you will remember that the objective was to observe how your mind bounced around from this thought to that thought to the next. The practice of functional mindfulness is very similar. In functional mindfulness, you don't change anything that you are doing, or are thinking about doing. You merely become aware of your actions, thoughts and intentions and make a note of them in much the same way that you noted them during the "monkey mind" exercise.

I should clarify just what "intended" means in this context. By way of example, I used to become quite agitated when drivers would go out of their way to behave disrespectfully to other motorists. When I observed this type of behavior, the "old me" wanted to roll down the window, shout something unpleasant at the offending driver, and maybe even direct a rather rude gesture in his direction. If I had been practicing functional mindfulness, I would simply have noticed that I had the intention of flipping off the driver even though I hadn't actually followed through on the intention.

Similarly, many business executives cannot make it through a day without experiencing the intention to tell a boss what he can do with his negative performance review or a customer that it's disrespectful to treat a supplier so rudely. In fact, the very nature of most corporate cultures and business enviornments gives rise to innumerable, unexpressed intentions. Because of political correctness, legal constraints, traditional hierarchical structures, and other factors, you can't simply say or do what you want. Thus, your intentions are many but your ability to act on them are often few.

The essential lesson here is that we place things into our minds through a variety of pathways: through what we say and do, what we think and what we intend. It doesn't matter which road the clutter takes to find its way in.

Last, be honest about what you create and place into your own mind every day. There's nothing to be ashamed of. You practice functional mindfulness in complete privacy. It is a tool of self-awareness. Many people are shocked by not only the number of times they engage in negative thoughts and actions, but also how often they were really angry at someone for something. Remember, awareness is the first step to resolution. Recall my earlier example about the man that completely misunderstood the reason I'd dropped my car off to be serviced. Before you can fix something, you need to know what is going on.

Exercise Three: Keep a Time/Mind/Source Journal

Unlike the meditation exercises previously discussed, you perform functional meditation simply by going about your daily business. The only task that needs to be added to your usual routine is keeping a detailed journal of what you did, thought and intended throughout the course of your day.

♦ This exercise requires that you keep a journal for the period that you practice functional mindfulness. Since this book is written for those with very busy schedules, keep the journal for only two consecutive days. The headings on this journal are simple: (1) Time. (2) I am mindful that: and (3) Source: "Source" is for you to make a notation of how the mindfulness came to your attention. Were you saying it to someone, thinking it, feeling it or even fantasizing about it? I had someone read me a journal entry once that said "8:15 a.m. I'm mindful that I'm fantasizing about killing my boss. Source: you might write here, "I actually muttered it under my breath" or possibly, "just a thought." This level of documentation is helpful in reviewing your journal because you'll learn just how far back in the chain of events you need to go to head off the clutter. If your entry says, "I was mindful that I lied to a colleague," and you note that the Source was "the act of lying to this person," it's a different challenge than just thinking about deceiving someone.

♦ It isn't necessary to walk around with the journal attached to your hip. On the other hand, it is not effective to try to summarize all of what you were mindful of when you get home at night. As much of a challenge as it is, I suggest that you take two minutes every half hour to jot your notes in your journal. Some people will jot their observations on notepads during slow stretches in meetings. Others prefer "verbal journals"—talking their mindful observations into tape recorders or other electronic devices. If necessary, plan brief but regular breaks for yourself during the day where you'll have a little time and privacy to record your thoughts, acts, and intentions. What is most crucial, though, is that you make a sincere effort to *be mindful* during this exercise. The idea is to become aware of what you're doing and thinking and make a brief entry about it.

♦ Do not review your journal regularly or even at the end of a day (We'll get to what you need to do with the journal shortly). As you perform this exercise, remember that most of us are not very aware of what we are doing or thinking as we go about our day. A lot of people are surprised – some are shocked – when they stop to become aware of what they are doing and thinking in much the same way I was when I recognized my insensitivity toward the gas station attendant. Whatever emerges, recognize that this came from inside of you. You needn't judge it, analyze it or try to rationalize it. Simply acknowledge it. It is quite possible that, after noting some of your feelings, actions and thoughts, you may decide to make some changes. If and when you do, those kinds of changes will end up making your active meditation much easier and more effective. In fact, it is the equivalent in meditation to a two day garage sale!

♦ On the second night after making entries into your functional mindfulness journal, set the journal aside without reviewing the entries. The process of performing functional mindfulness is often a stressful one. To offset this stress go back to the "mindfulness of breath" exercise at the end of Chapter Two and perform that exercise. Your goal is to rest and collect your emotional energy.

Troubleshooting

People that encounter difficulties in functional mindfulness usually fall into one of two groups. The first group has a fundamental misunderstanding of what mindfulness actually is. It is more than just verbally acknowledging what one is doing or thinking. It involves making oneself consciously aware of it. It is not enough simply to *say*, "I'm mindful that I'm frustrated with my boss." You must go beyond just saying the words and take one or two seconds to internalize what that frustration feels like.

The second group has difficulty because they try to side-step the time that it takes to log the journal entries.

A few years ago, a great entrepreneur asked me to teach him meditation. Since he didn't want anyone to know what he was up to, I agreed to instruct him privately and, because we both travel for business and often found ourselves in different parts of the country, I sometimes instructed him by phone.

When it became time to introduce him to functional mindfulness, he hit a major roadblock. Since functional mindfulness requires us to take note of what we're doing as we do it, this entrepreneur resisted investing the time required because it intruded on his hectic schedule. He kept insisting that he was perfectly able to summarize for me at the end of any day exactly what he'd done every moment of that day. He also objected to the exercise as "completely unproductive." Thinking back to the calm, serene approach that I knew Dzongsar would have taken with me had I leveled such an objection, I calmly asked him what he would do if he found out that someone was dumping toxic waste in the back of his office building. Without detailing his somewhat colorful response, I will tell you that, he emphatically stated he would see that such activity was stopped immediately.

By communicating that his being unmindful of what was going into his attic was no different than dumping toxic waste into his own head, he agreed to keep a journal of his mindfulness for one day. I called to see how he was doing in the middle of the day. When he replied with an ebullient, "Fine, no problems!" I began to wonder if he was actually doing the exercise as I had asked.

I asked him to read me the last few entries in his journal. I heard some papers shuffling and he read: "11:20; now I'm telling my accountant that he's a fu****** idiot. 11:38; now I'm mindful that I'm telling my sales manager that he can't find his ass with both hands. 11:40 now I'm mindful that I just told one of our suppliers to shove…" At least he was honest.

It seems that my toxic waste example had been more relevant than I had known. Needless to say, it took some time for me convince the entrepreneur that quieting the mind is a very difficult task when such disrespectful debris is being tossed around daily.

If you are experiencing similar resistance to functional mindfulness, ask yourself:

♦ What would you be willing to do if someone was ruining you life, or your business?

♦ If corporate counsel came to you and said, "Look, we can win this case and you'll end up with a million dollar bonus; all you need to do is write down what you were doing or thinking every half hour for two days," what do you think you'd do?

The benefits you will gain through the practice of functional mindfulness will have a much greater impact on your life than winning a million dollar bonus ever could. Just ask any executive that is genuinely dedicated to meditation.

Chapter Four
- Inventory Reduction Sale -

The functional mindfulness exercise, if executed properly, usually produces a moderate psychological or spiritual jolt. When you become conscious of what is going on in your mind, you receive a mild shock of recognition. Though some people receive a more severe jolt, most of you won't have a negative experience. At worst, you may feel a bit unsettled.

If you do feel unsettled, take a day or two off from the meditation schedule and revert to the mindfulness of breath meditation practice detailed at the end of Chapter Two. You should practice mindfulness of breath, at a minimum, in the mornings and in the evenings. This practice is very calming and should be performed more often if needed to regain a sense of balance. By quieting the mind, you'll also find time to adjust to what your conscious and subconscious minds are up to.

When you feel ready to proceed, begin to process the significance of the information in your journal. You have created an inventory of your running mind and have likely garnered some insight into just how much clutter you allow into your attic every day. Mindfulness has now illustrated for you what is going on in your mind as you go about your daily routine.

Anyone who has performed this exercise and is *not* surprised at the results should probably proceed directly to the Himalayas and assume the Lotus position. Any such person already has achieved a state of mindfulness far more advanced than most of the monks in the mountains. At the very least, most people are shocked at all the junk they manage to cram into their brains. You were probably also surprised at how many different entries you made in your journal. Research psychologists have done studies and determined that many people have as many as 1,000 thoughts an hour!

With your journal as your guide, you can create a "sentry" to exert some control over what you toss into your attic. This is also a good opportunity to look at some of the thoughts and behaviors you've documented and decide what you might want to change. Acute awareness of your behaviors helps you become calmer and more even-tempered, translating into improved interpersonal relationships. In fact, research shows that improvement in virtually all kinds of relationships – personal and professional – is nearly universal as meditation practice is integrated into a person's life.

This is especially important for business executives who have tried and failed to become relationship-driven managers. In most major organizations, high potential executives are asked to go through training programs and one-on-one coaching to become more "people-oriented." Typically, these high potentials have superior skills and knowledge but fall down when it comes to working in teams. They excel as individual performers but don't communicate well or seem incapable of showing empathy. Though meditation isn't a panacea, it does offer a relationship-building alternative—and one that is less costly and time-consuming than coaching or formal training.

Lesson 4: Taking Stock

Think of your mindfulness journal as a sacred and deeply personal item. You don't have to share it – any part of it – with anyone. I have yet to meet a person who doesn't have at least a few things about themselves that they would not want published on the front page of the local newspaper. Try to keep in mind the reasons that you have decided to explore meditation in the first place. It is likely that you were seeking some level of change in your life, a way to calm your mind and become a less stressed and a more authentic human being. If you're like most professionals, you've become interested in meditation as a way to deal with the intense pressure involved in just about every field and industry.

No matter why you have decided to explore meditation, please keep in mind that you are bound to evolve as you become increasingly mindful. Accept the journey for what it is and try not to be too hard on your self.

Chris, a man in his late 30s, did not initially accept the journey. On the surface, Chris seemed very much together and at ease. He joined one of my beginning meditation practices, ostensibly so that he could accompany his girlfriend, who was eager to learn meditation.

As we went through the first several sessions, I had the impression that this man, we'll call him Chris, was barely going through the motions and was not taking the assignments very seriously. As we approached the session where I begin to talk about the functional mindfulness practice, I found an opportunity to speak with him alone for a moment and attempted to get him more personally involved with the process.

I told Chris that his girlfriend was probably going to have a bit of a challenge with this part of the program and that it might really help her if *he* dug in and applied all of his obvious intellect and effort to the exercise. I added that he could then explain it to her later on. He assured me with a kind of twisted sincerity that he'd complete the exercise as directed and "show her how it's done."

It's always interesting for me to study the faces of people as this particular part of the course is explained. I then compare those expressions to the ones they have when they return a few days later after having completed the functional mindfulness exercise. No less than 75% of the people look like they've had some serious air let out of their balloons. In this case I took very careful note of Chris' expression as he strutted out of the group session that evening.

Three days later, as everyone was filing back in, I noted that Chris looked like he'd lost his best friend, his dog, his sanity and his girlfriend all in one day. Recognizing that people with some overt arrogance are often very sensitive about being embarrassed, I said nothing but instead kept an eye on him as I went around the room asking for people to share their general experiences with the functional mindfulness exercise. Just as I called on his girlfriend, Chris got up and walked out of the room.

I caught up with Chris sitting outside during one of our breaks. He was smoking a cigarette and seemed quite shaken. Without making a big deal out of it, I sat down next to him on the stairs and asked if everything was okay.

"I am the worst person in the entire world," he responded. I assured him that he was not and asked if he was willing to share what part of the mindfulness exercise had triggered this negative perception. "You can't possibly understand," he said. "You're this guy that goes around helping everyone that he meets and I am literally the opposite," he continued, his voice quivering now. I assured him that, like him, I was quite human and that we probably both had very similar things in life that we regretted. That seemed to set him at ease.

I listened to Chris list some of his "transgressions." Most were nothing out of the ordinary. The shock for Chris was that his arrogance and his ego had always assured him that he was an okay guy, probably even better than just okay. He had managed to block out any of his less than ideal behaviors in life by practicing the exact opposite of mindfulness. Chris may as well have gone through his average day saying to himself, "Now I am *oblivious* that I am acting like a jerk. Now I am **oblivious** that I am being arrogant."

Chris had a decent position in middle-management working within the retail industry, and the pressures that his job created, the sheer velocity at which the world came at Chris every moment of every day, didn't allow him the luxury of a free moment to reflect or a sustained period of peace and quiet. In addition, Chris spent every extra cent he had on trying to make his girlfriend happy, ratcheting up the pressure he put on himself. No wonder he relied on ego and arrogance to get him through the day. Chris was capable of resolving these issues on his own without meditation, but he lived and worked in a world of perpetual noise, preventing him from really hearing what he needed to hear.

Chris took the exercise in functional mindfulness to heart. He worked on it for several months, until *he* felt that he had documented all of the stylistic elements in his behavior that he believed he needed to improve. Chris reached the conclusion that those behaviors and the style with which he conducted himself prevented him from achieving a calm state; that his only chance for peace of mind resided in altering those behaviors.

It took Chris almost two years to make the most essential changes. I watched him transform himself from his self-described "worst person in the world" to someone that embraced compassion and empathy as a way of life. His career soared as he became a master at managing relationships in truly brilliant and creative ways. He married his girlfriend, and Chris now spends several hours a week teaching basic meditation to anyone who wants to learn.

Exercise #4: Learning from Journaling

Don't become hung up on negative behaviors as you do this journal exercise. The point of it isn't to make you feel badly about actions that you're not particularly proud of or to catalyze immediate behavioral changes. While you may want to consider changing certain aspects of yourself—being more reflective in tense work situations, giving your employees the benefits of the doubt and so on—you should make these changes only if and when you feel they're called for. Don't use this exercise as an excuse to make changes you don't really want to make (or that you're not ready for).

Instead, recognize and then reiterate out loud that you are in fact human and that part of being human means you're going to make a certain number of mistakes. I also recommend that you perform 10 to 15 minutes of "mindfulness of breath" meditation prior to going through the process of reviewing your journal. That should take you to a place of calm and balance prior to dealing with this challenge.

♦ After meditating, study the various entries in your mindfulness journal.

♦ Try to pick the top three or four items in your journal that probably brought about feelings of discord in you or in those around you. An entry such as "3:48 p.m.: slammed the door on the V.P. of Marketing because he *still* refuses to do things my way" is the kind of entry that should grab your attention. What you're looking for are entries that describe situations where people became uneasy or even outright angry. Place those in a separate "priority resolutions" list.

♦ Take some time to study your priority resolutions list. Go back in your mind to the events that triggered the notes in your journal. Without thinking at all about who was right or wrong in those scenarios, ask yourself what your day **would** have been like without this event? Envision how the entire day would have gone had X, Y or Z not even occurred. Obviously, if you had a serious disagreement with your spouse as you left for work that day, this unpleasant event probably colored your mood and may have even catalyzed some of the negative things that occurred at work. What if you had been mindful of all of this throughout the day? How would your subsequent journal entries have been different? How would your day have been different had you not behaved or talked in a way that precipitated discord?

♦ Spend the next two days studying your journal list in an effort to identify the top few items that, if you had been practicing mindfulness full time, would have played out differently. Look at each thing you did or didn't do, each thought you had, each intention that you didn't act on, and visualize the ensuing chain of events that ultimately led to discord in your life. As you become more mindful of how your thoughts and actions impact subsequent events, concentrate on being more aware of how what you say and do can create discord; try and reduce or eliminate these words and deeds from your standard operating procedure.

Precisely how you choose to manage the resolution of the items in your journal is up to you. Most people notice greatly improved relationships and increased inner calm if they deal with just the top three or four items in their inventory. Others decide to make an earnest attempt to extend this work to a deeper level.

When I was learning this practice, I developed a technique called the "three second hard stop." It is a very effective behavior modification technique, and you may want to make it a part of your operating style. The practice of the three second stop involves evoking a mechanism of self-control *before* responding to someone. For three seconds, you ponder the impact of a possible action before you actually proceed with what you intended to do or.

In learning the practice of the three second stop, you will very quickly progress to a point where you recognize — in advance — which "intersections" require you to employ the technique and which do not. Some situations are similar to a four-way intersection on a country road where you can see for miles in all directions; then you can act without hesitation. On the other hand, if you were approaching a five-way intersection with two gas tankers and three cars at all the other points of the compass, taking those few seconds to think through whether you want to proceed through the intersection in the way planning is a very good idea.

Sometimes that three seconds can save you from problems that are contingent on a future developments. In other words, you can stop the future from developing in this problematic direction by using these three seconds wisely. Give yourself these three seconds and practice using them. As the "hard stop" becomes integrated into your functional style, you'll find that fewer people are telling you, "We've got a problem." These three seconds can stop you from triggers in all sorts of business crises. When you fire someone in anger, the three second stop will save you from uttering the words that results in an employee discrimination lawsuit. In those three seconds, you may reconsider your decision to ignore a customer request—avoidance that may very well cost you the customer's account. Or you may use those three seconds to prevent yourself from speaking harshly to your boss, and he won't have those harsh words in his mind when he's deciding whether to give you a promotion.

Troubleshooting

After learning from journaling, your ego may have trouble accepting your imperfections. When I first went though this exercise, I was so shocked at some of the things I was doing that I sat down and wrote a dozen or so letters to people in an attempt to mend fences and apologize for my actions.

As I've pointed out, mindfulness is an essential meditative practice. There is no time clock running and you needn't feel pressured to solve all of your issues in one day or even one week. If you note something on your list and you decide you want to change that behavior or process of thinking, allow yourself some time to do so.

Try to work on one item at a time; don't try to remake your entire style all at once. Just remember, the idea here is to quiet the mind by placing less clutter in the attic. If you're doing something – anything – that you recognize as unproductive, how much longer do you feel you need to keep doing it before you'll simply give up on hoping for a different result?

Change takes time. That is never more true than when we are trying to change something about ourselves. If you're having trouble here, be patient and keep at it. Eventually you will establish a sentry that will keep your mind's clutter to a minimum and, when that happens, some of the behaviors that you have identified as undesirable will begin to disappear.

Case Study #4-1: Meditate or Medicate?

Cindy, a middle-aged senior executive, who had tremendous corporate responsibilities that brought about inordinate amounts of stress in her life, decided to learn to meditate. She had decided to try meditation at the suggestion of her doctor, who had become quite concerned that she was developing a dependency on Valium, which at the time was her chosen method of coping with corporate stress.

Cindy started and stopped her instruction in basic meditation several times, always using the excuse that she had no time in her schedule to come to class, much less fit in the 15 minutes twice a day to do the practices. As she was about to drop the group for the third time, I told her that I'd endorse her leaving if she would commit to doing one exercise for one hour. She agreed.

I outlined the exercise in functional mindfulness and told her that she had to do the journal part of the exercise exactly as described. She informed me in no uncertain terms that she was perfectly aware of what went on in her mind at all times. She insisted that she could sit down right then and write an entire day's mindfulness journal for me. I wasn't crazy about the idea, since I know that people leave out about 95% of the behaviors that are least attractive when they take this shortcut. Still, I sensed that it was now or never for Cindy. There was little chance that she'd continue with the meditation class if I refused her request.

After the group had cleared out for the night, I handed her a few sheets of paper and proceeded to explain the details of the exercise. "Now, Cindy, you have to take yourself back in your mind to those moments that you're writing about. You have to say, 'now I am mindful that I am…whatever' and actually *think* about what you were really thinking and doing just then."

She made some kind of flippant remark as I handed her a pen and told her to have at it. Less than a minute after she started writing, I noticed that her hand was trembling. Two minutes later I saw the tears rolling down her face and a few seconds after that, this tough senior executive simply exploded in a sobbing jag. I went to get her some tea and tissues so that she could have some time to regain her composure.

When I came back, I asked her what was wrong. "I absolutely cannot believe what a total bitch I am to people that work for me," she let out. "It's not just some of them some of the time, it's all of them virtually *all* of the time," she went on.

Without saying anything I simply nodded my head and allowed her to think about her revelation.

I didn't want to seem insensitive but I have learned that there is a tremendous difference between verbally acknowledging our behaviors and going through the process of attesting to them for oneself by writing them down. When I told Cindy that she needed to put this on paper so that she could think about it later on, she resisted at first but finally agreed. After she wrote the description of her behavior in her own words, she sat there staring at it for quite a while.

Finally, I asked her what she was doing and she responded without hesitation, "I'm thinking about what it must feel like to be on the receiving end of all the stuff I put these people through." That was the moment of true change for her. A year or so later she told me that that this had been the exact moment when every relationship in her life began to improve. She had been forced to start viewing things from the point of view of those that she affected.

Even if she hadn't completed basic meditation classes — which she did, and ended up by far being the most dedicated student in the group — her overall stress level still would have dropped. She went from literally screeching at everyone on her staff all day long to a person who came through the door in the morning asking if she could help *them* in some way.

Her home life transformed itself as well. Instead of a person engaged in battle from the moment she left the house in the morning to the time she returned at night, she became someone that left and came home relatively calm and peaceful. What do you think happened in her home life? How would your life change if stress and tension were reduced just by half in your daily life?

Today, Cindy is happier and more at peace and, incidentally, so are most of the people in her life, all because she took the few minutes to take a simple inventory and be mindful of what she was doing, thinking and feeling as she went through her normal daily affairs. She says she became a far better and more effective executive and actually made better decisions because she had a base level calmness from which to make such decisions.

Chapter Five
- Quarterly Report -

Just as you might do with business objectives, stand back and assess what progress you have made so far and identify what issues might need greater focus. At this juncture, you should be getting more comfortable with the mindfulness of breath practice. Just as significantly, you should be relying on this practice when stress mounts or when you're functioning below par for whatever reason.

After successfully completing the functional mindfulness journal exercise, you'll probably enter a phase where you begin to question how you manage your daily activities and virtually all of your relationships as well. This may mean that you'll become much more critical of the way you relate to a particular customer, for instance. You may wonder if your unwillingness to be completely honest and open with him is right. You may even question whether your particular management style dovetails with the culture and policies of your organization.

As you learn to meditate more effectively and begin to experiment with other methods, progressively integrate greater levels of mindfulness into your daily routine. Some people prefer to practice mindfulness on the drive to and from work. A meditation student of mine recently told me that since he began regularly practicing mindfulness on his drive to work, he has started each day with much greater serenity than in the past.

This student is executing an extremely dynamic form of meditation that serves to distract and quiet the mind. In addition, he's no longer spending his drive time chattering away on his cell phone and becoming enmeshed in business problems before he's even reached his office. Now, when he arrives at work, his head is completely clear and he enjoys a true sense of balance. The alternative is to hit the elevator agitated, aggravated and off-balance.

I'm not suggesting that you toss your cell phone out the window (although that suggestion may seem attractive to you) and do nothing but practice mindfulness day in and day out. Integrating meditation into a professional (and personal) life is about finding balance. It's up to you to find out precisely where that point of balance is, and locating this point is an ongoing process.

Maybe 10 minutes of meditation twice a day results in a satisfactory level of inner peace for you. As you progress more deeply into meditation, you may discover that increasing your meditation time is desirable. More than one executive has told me that they've been more than willing to make the tradeoff of time for peace and balance. Still, it's up to you to find the tradeoff that meets your particular needs.

For me, regularly practicing mindfulness lead to a period of intense introspection.

The more I meditated, the clearer my vision became. I began to see that no matter what I achieved or how I loaded up on my bank accounts and stock portfolio, I couldn't take that with me. I saw with shocking clarity that ATM machines didn't exist in whatever form of reality comes after this life. Once that particular realization hit home, my priorities began to shift. I became acutely mindful of what would extend beyond this life: my relationships with those I loved and cared about, whether I was compassionate or insensitive and so forth.

Even though I continued my corporate career for several years after this realization, my growing introspective nature gradually took me on a journey of spiritual questioning and insight.

I realized that my corporate life consumed so much of my time and energy that there was no more "me." All of my relationships had either failed or been severely compromised because I was so completely focused on business. In fact, eventually my introspection led me on a spiritual journey. As I became an increasingly spiritual person, I abandoned my entire corporate life. I surrendered my directorships and turned in my keys to the executive washroom.

This journey is chronicled in my book, *Beyond the Broken Gate* and may serve as a resource, describing how what you learn in meditation can take you on a spiritual awakening. While my awakening took an extraordinary form, it's possible that your journey can be extraordinary in a different way, one that fits your particular set of experiences and goals.

As you reflect upon these ideas, don't panic if you're uncertain about how intensely or frequently you should engage in these meditative practices. Give yourself permission to take a day, a week or even longer to be introspective and reach a point where you're clear about what you need to do. As you go through this period of introspection, practice the mindfulness of breath exercise at least twice a day so that you continue to quiet your mind.

Lesson 5: Assessing Your Progress

Directors, CEOs, corporate officers and managers recognize the importance of periodic assessment as a tool to help plot their forward business course. In the same way, you need to assess your progress before continuing on with this spiritual journey. Therefore, revisit the monkey mind exercise in order to see how far you have come and to help plan a course for moving forward.

The meditation practices that we'll be exploring in the ensuing chapters require greater degrees of concentration than earlier exercises That's why you need to do an assessment of the foundation you've built and determine if it will allow you to concentrate more intently in the future.

Exercise 5: Monkey Mind Redux

As you'll recall, this exercise is called, "observing the monkey mind." The objective here is to perform the exercise exactly as you did on the first day but to note any changes that might have occurred since you started meditating.

Again, it is literally impossible to do anything incorrectly in performing this particular exercise because you're simply observing how your mind functions. The exercise takes ten minutes at this stage and needs to be done once in the morning.

♦ You'll need a piece of paper and something to write with. Go to the place you have chosen for quiet meditation. Close the doors, unplug the phones and do whatever it takes to achieve a peaceful environment. And get comfortable. Make sure you have a clock or a watch so that you can note the time at various junctures in the exercise.

♦ Now, make a note of your "start time." Close your eyes and try to clear your mind completely. Quiet your mind gently, clear it of all thoughts and forget all things that are currently occupying your mind. Allow it to go wherever it wants to go of its own momentum.

♦ Observe and take mental note of what comes into your thoughts. This must be done without judgment or criticism. You are **not** failing if you still have difficulty focusing your mind. Your job is to observe what comes into your thoughts and simply note it. There's no such thing as a good or bad thought here. Just note exactly what comes in.

♦ Continue to observe the thoughts, ideas and feelings that come into your mind – no matter what they are – for what you think is about ten minutes. When you feel that ten minutes has passed, open your eyes. Look at the clock, write down the "end time."

♦ Now, write down as many of the thoughts, ideas, and feelings as you can. Include everything you experienced, whatever came into your mind as you attempted to quiet your thoughts. Be sure to write down everything, no matter how insignificant it might seem.

For the evening practice on this day, take the 10 or 15 minutes allocated for meditation and study the outcome of your morning practice. Review your notations and consider these questions:

♦ Were your efforts to quiet the mind any more effective than the first time you performed the monkey mind exercise?

♦ How did the experience compare to the first time you performed it? Did different subjects emerge? Were you more aware of the thoughts coming into your mind?

♦ Were you able to pass the time without becoming frustrated or "fidgety?" How does this compare to last time?

If you noticed no difference at all between your two exeriences, go back and perform the basic exercise at the end of Chapter One a few times until you become more comfortable with the process of documenting what goes on in your mind when you attempt to silence it. When you do so, be acutely observant of what transpires while you attempt to quiet your mind. If you have to go back to this basic exercise, don't feel as if you've failed or are incapable of meditation. We all master different practices at different speeds, and for whatever reason, you simply need to repeat this particular one. It's similar to how some work tasks are easy for you and some are more difficult.

On the other hand, if you have noted a discernable degree of improvement in your ability to quiet your mind and document your thoughts, you're right on track. You've begun to make significant progress in tempering your internal dialogue.

Troubleshooting

Most of the changes that people experience in the first nine or ten days of learning meditation are subtle. Chances are very good that if you have followed the course as it has been laid out in this book, you have made progress, even if it's not readily apparent.

If you truly feel that there was no real change between the first time and the second time you did the exercise or that it was more difficult to quiet your mind this time, then you may be trying too hard. Remember, meditation is not a feat of strength – not even of mental strength. It is an orchestration of finesse.

One other potential obstacle to making progress in the earliest stages of learning meditation involves the "klaxon lead-in." Business people often lead lives that are tantamount to standing next to a klaxon going off at full blast all day long: Phones ringing, computers beeping, customers screaming, bosses demanding and direct reports complaining—the cacophony combined with its non-stop nature can make it difficult to transition to a meditative state.

Here is an interim step that will help dim your recollection of the noise of the day. It will provide a needed segue from the tumult of your office to the peaceful state of meditation. To help you grasp this interim step, let me share with you the story of how I slowly learned to glide into the process of going quiet.

Many years ago, when I was having difficulty adopting a certain meditation practice that required great subtlety and finesse, Dzongsar instructed me to visualize standing directly next to a gigantic waterfall that was hundreds of feet high. He told me to attune my hearing to the highest level and hear every bit of the deafening sound as the water came crashing down.

After I could hear the sounds of the waterfall in my mind, Dzongsar instructed me to imagine that I was slowly walking away from the waterfall. As I did so, the sound of the waterfall softened. Dzongsar guided me carefully through this exercise, urging me to focus on the sounds of the falling water. As I followed his instruction and "moved" farther away from the waterfall, I could actually "hear" the volume of the crashing water decrease.

Before I knew it, Dzongsar had gently shifted from "walking" me away from the waterfall into the guided meditation that I had been having so much trouble with previously.

If you find yourself having difficulty holding focus either at the point described within Exercise 5 or at any other juncture along your pathway of learning a given meditation practice, try this "calming waterfall" visualization practice.

As you become more proficient at the practices described in these pages, you will be able to slide into meditative balance much quicker and deeper than you are able to right now.

Chapter Six
- Focus Please -

At this point, you have begun to establish some basic skills in meditation. It is likely that you have also confronted some challenges that might be holding you back. Hopefully, you are now comfortable with the mindfulness of breath practice and are realizing some of the calming benefits of that meditation technique. Now it's time to move on to the second type of essential practice, focused meditation.

Focused meditation is what most people envision when they think of meditation. In their mind's eye, they see a yogi sitting in the Lotus position, chanting complex mantras[3] in Sanskrit as he drifts into a trance. While certain deep focus practices are known to evoke remarkable altered states, I very much doubt that anyone reading this book will start levitating any time soon.

[3]*mantra / Man' tra/ n. (Sanskrit)*
(1) A sacred verbal formula repeated in prayer, meditation or incantation such as an invocation of a god, a magic spell or a syllable or portion of scripture containing mystical potentialities. (2) A prayer, invocation; a religious charm

Focused meditation is a practice where we direct the mind to concentrate intently on one particular thing. That "thing" can be a mantra, a Hindu word meaning "to petition through execution of a sacred word or phrase," an image, such as an icon that would evoke a feeling of peace and tranquility (Buddha, Vishnu, Jesus are a few examples), a candle, or anything else that facilitates intense focus for a given period of time.

While the most orthodox meditation teachers limit what can be used as focal points, experience has taught me that focused meditation works best if each person is allowed to experiment with different focal practices. I was initially instructed to practice focal meditation through mantra repetition but found that I reached a meditative state much more readily if I focused on the rhythm of ocean waves as they rolled ashore. This method, however, doesn't work for everybody. Some people find themselves distracted by passersby or by the mere fact that their eyes are open. Using a candle as a focal point can pose additional challenges. Many people who start out in focused meditation using a candle end up reaching a state of self-hypnosis, rather than deep meditation.

Rather than create a lengthy list of potential focal items, I will defer to the wisdom of the ages – and the sages – and direct readers toward a mantra for now. At the end of this chapter I will list a number of alternatives that you can experiment with as primary items of focus for this type of practice.

Focused meditation produces a different experience than the practices that have been outlined thus far. Even though the exercises may *seem* a lot like the mindfulness of breath practice, focusing in this new way sometimes produces challenges. Achieving the desired results might take just a bit more dedication.

In focused meditation, recognize that there are times when you simply will not feel like performing the stages and steps that are necessary to execute the exercises. If and when this happens, allow yourself the latitude to say, "I am just not going to do this right now." The worst thing you could do is try to force yourself to meditate.

Lesson 6: Finding Your Mantra

Focused meditation involves actively focusing your mind on some specific item while at the same time allowing your mind to relax completely. While this may seem like a paradox, here's how to resolve it. Just consider what occurs when you are focusing intently on some work project. Before you know it, you look up and are shocked that two hours have elapsed. This is analogous to the focused meditation experience.

In the Graybar Method, focused meditation is practiced in progressive stages. The process incorporates a sequence of techniques to "step down" the activity of the brain and begin the process of temporary desensitization of the mind. When you reach progressively more deeply into that process, you're left with nothing but the pure essence and natural, quiet perfection of oneness. I've observed professional football players shed tears of joy and a stressed-out executive so relaxed that she became as loose as a jellyfish.

You will need to decide on a mantra that will be your point of focus. Some "New Age" devotees have been instructed that a mantra must be very personalized and given to them by a master after a period of deep contemplation. Devotees of strict Transcendental Meditation insist that in order to properly practice focused meditation, one needs a four-syllable mantra designed so that the accent is on a specific syllable. Any mantra that helps you sharpen your focus and retain your attention over the meditation interval, however, is a good one. I know a very devoted Catholic who has found great success using the "Hail Mary" as a mantra.

Since this book is specifically geared toward people who are new to meditation practices, the mantras that will be suggested here are fairly simple. You are, of course, free to select your own mantra so long as you understand that the purpose of a mantra is to create a focal point that induces comfort and peace. It can be one word or a short combination of a few words that contain a rhythm you find pleasant. If pronouncing or repeating the mantra is too complex or challenging, it's not a good mantra for you.

Here are a few sample mantras that have stood the test of time.

> **OM** – This is pronounced "ooh mmmm" with the mmmm aspect of the mantra being extended for a few seconds. The mantra is repeated over and over either just under the breath or, if you are comfortable, slightly louder. The belief is that chanting this mantra and slightly extending the "mmmmm" portion of it creates an interesting resonance that is felt internally while being heard. This combination is supposed to have positive effects on the chakras[4].

> **OM Namah Shivaya** – This mantra is pronounced "Ooh mmm, Nah Ma She' Vah Ya." When enunciated, the "Ooh mmm" portion of the mantra is sustained for roughly two of the four counts with the other two syllables assigned one count each. For those seeking a bit more than just the repetition of one sound and who need some cadence to help focus their attention, this mantra is very simple and effective. The origin of this Hindu mantra is a recognition of the first six chakras. It roughly translates as "a salute to that which I may ultimately become."

---

[4]*Chakra / ch^k' rah / n. (Sanskrit)*
(1) One of the seven centers of spiritual energy in the human body according to yogi philosophy. (2) Wheel, circle.

Om Mani Padme Hum – Pronounced "Oooh mah knea padma hoom," this is one of the more famous short mantras. (Some are as many as 100 syllables, but we'll skip those for now.) This mantra has its roots in Tibetan Buddhism and the essence of its meaning is that when the mind and heart become united, anything is possible. By far, this is the most practiced mantra in the world today.

Exercise 6: Focused Meditation

This type of focused meditation requires a bit more of your time. After you become more proficient in focused meditation, you will most likely find that you can accomplish what you need to in 15 minutes, twice a day. For now, though, it may take an extra five minutes twice a day until you acclimate to these practices.

If we had the luxury of conducting this lesson in a class setting, this would be the point where I would put down my notes, sit in a chair with the rest of the group and begin what Dzongsar would call a "heart instruction." Meditation, at least the aspects of it that will be practiced from here forward, is more than simply going through the motions and chanting mantras. In order for meditation to work, you must adopt a sincere attitude toward the practice. Meditation requires more from you than invoking a quick "Power of Positive Thinking" affirmation. You must believe that the process of meditation *will* lead you within the very essence of who you are and toward your goals.

♦ Go to the quiet place that you have chosen to do your meditation and take all the steps possible to assure an uninterrupted 20 minutes.

♦ You will realize better results from focused meditation if you formally acknowledge to yourself that this is a time that you have chosen to meditate. I begin my practice with a silent "I want and need to meditate now," and I've found that this expression results in noticeably more effective sessions then when I skip this step. Also, think about whether you feel like meditating. If the answer is no, allow yourself the freedom to say, "I just don't want to do this right now." Do not force it.

♦ Before beginning any overt practice, allow yourself to become aware of your surroundings. Increase your sensitivity and awareness of what the room you are in "feels" like and what you "feel" like at that moment. Don't analyze or judge these things, just let yourself become more acutely aware of them.

♦ Begin this exercise by performing the mindfulness of breath practice. This time, though, don't use the peaceful or restful vision imagery that you have previously employed. Your sole focus is on becoming mindful of breathing in and breathing out. You must focus solely on the breath and the cadence of your breathing. Your goal is to reach a deep recognition that it is *you* breathing. Your awareness of that breath is an awareness of yourself. Practice this variation of mindfulness of breath for about five minutes.

♦ Make a subtle transition from performing the mindfulness of breath practice into beginning your mantra. Imagine that you are standing on the top rung of a 20-step ladder. The mindfulness of breath practice is designed to initially calm the mind down a few levels to, say, the sixteenth rung. By the time you complete this practice in focused meditation, you will have brought your mind down to possibly the 12th rung. It may take several days of practice to accomplish a smooth transition from being mindful of breath to performing your mantra. Don't get frustrated. Take your time in learning how to make this transition.

♦ When you begin your mantra, start slowly and work upwards to a rhythm and pace that is comfortable. If you have a type "A" personality, guard against turning into a contest to see how many times you can repeat the mantra in the next 10 or 12 minutes. You will have achieved the best possible balance in repeating your mantra when you are aware of every syllable without being aware of having to recollect every syllable. Dzongsar instructed me early on to "enter into and become" the mantra. If you achieve this, take it as a sign of significant proficiency in this practice. If you don't achieve it, however, it doesn't mean you've failed. What's crucial is reaching a state where your only conscious "activity" is repeating the mantra over and over at a cadence that is neither contrived nor overly accelerated. Perform the mantra practice and be mindful that you are performing the mantra. Think of the story we were told as children about the "little train that could"and the train's repeated, "I think I can, I think I can." This spirit and cadence is appropriate for a mantra exercise.

♦ When you first begin, allot aproximately 10 to 12 minutes for focused meditation (above and beyond the portion where you are performing the mindfulness of breath practice). As you progress to a point where you make the transition from the mindfulness of breath practice to the focused practice more easily, reduce the mindfulness of breath portion to three minutes and adjust the focused practice to to about 12 minutes so that your overall practice is 15 minutes. Naturally, if you are getting a lot of benefit from this particular practice, you can extend it to 30 minutes.

Practice focused meditation twice a day for the next two weeks. It is an essential meditation practice and your first foray into the process of integrating one practice form into another. In the Graybar method, integration of methods is crucial to weaving the overall practice together. Therefore, make sure you take the time to master this technique.

To increase your business performance and achieve significant levels of inner peace, you don't have to achieve the meditation level of the most serious practitioners. The practices described here, therefore, are designed to help you achieve goals tied to performance and inner peace rather than more ambitious spiritual goals. The following list of objectives will tell you if you're making good progress in the focal meditation portion of this method after one or two weeks of practice:

♦ A generalized feeling of well-being or ease that extends beyond the time that you are engaging in "active" meditation. The purpose of meditation is to extend the benefits beyond the periods that you are sitting in meditation.

♦ An increased willingness to tolerate the behaviors, actions and what might be perceived as "mistakes" of those around you. The concept of "resilient" often takes on new meaning as you progress more deeply into this level of practice.

♦ An ever-evolving sense of stability and poise. When I learned to meditate, I recall very clearly that, after about three weeks of practice, I simply became aware that the top 15% and the bottom 15% or so of the "mood swings" I might experience throughout the course of a day no longer had much of an effect. If I got angry about something, it wasn't nearly as virulent as it was prior to beginning meditation.

If you do not notice these kinds of changes, be patient. As I mentioned early on, the benefits that accrue from meditation are often subtle, in both practice and results. Stay with it and don't be surprised if someone else is the first to comment on how you've changed.

Troubleshooting

Beginning or extending the practice of intense meditation sometimes brings about a wide range of unexpected results. Most often, these outcomes are beneficial to such a degree that practitioners ask themselves why they waited so long to begin meditation.

In other cases, as the mind is quieted through the process of meditation, past events, traumas, personal issues and other life challenges may rise to the surface since you're no longer consistently using your mind's energy to suppress them. Here is just one example – and not as uncommon as you might suspect – of what can happen.

Case Study 6-1: A Silent Haunting Past

Jill, 35, asked if she could join a small impromptu group who had asked me to share some basic meditation pointers with them. At that time, I never asked even the most basic questions about an individual's background before working with them. I've since learned the importance of determining if the person has a history of depression, has experienced a recent trauma, has a serious mental health history or has some other type of serious issue. While these issues are not necessarily, in and of themselves, an absolute barrier to learning to meditate, they can produce intense feelings that may need to be addressed in another setting. This woman, however, gave every appearance of being well adjusted and normal in every way. She seemed more the "girl next door" than anything else.

After this group had met a couple of times, I noticed that Jill was a bit on the quiet side. I made a passing mental note of it and simply continued on with the instruction. We had just reached the point where I was beginning to discuss the elements of the focused meditation practices and, since we weren't pressed for time, I covered the entire topic that one night even though my usual custom was to break the lesson up into two sessions. I sent everyone home with the complete set of practices that would allow them to segue from mindfulness of breath into the focused meditation. I'd even assigned everyone a mantra based upon what I perceived to be their level of interest.

At the next session, I noticed that Jill hadn't shown up but didn't think much of it. I knew that she often traveled for business and assumed that she was out of town. When she again didn't show up, though, I asked one of the people in the group to call her and see if she had decided to drop out.

As it turned out, Jill had experienced a series of dreams and waking "events" where she recollected incidents of sexual abuse from her childhood. These events were so incredibly traumatic that she had blocked them from her conscious awareness. It was only as she began to truly quiet her mind through meditation practice that these events rose to the "reachable" portions of her conscious mind. As a result, she went through a very difficult period of having to deal with theose events from her past.

Fortunately, Jill had the maturity and common sense to seek counseling. I learned several months later that she was doing well in moving through these issues.

+   +   +

If you encounter any type of emotional or psychological difficulty while you are learning meditation, stop the practices immediately and resolve any issues before attempting further meditation. Do not hesitate to seek professional help. Each of us has experienced events and traumas that we probably would prefer to forget, and it's nothing to be ashamed of if they surface while learning meditation. After working through the issues and only after you have received an "all clear" from a therapist or other qualified professional, resume your practice. You will likely have to start at or near the beginning again, but you will benefit from your past experience with meditation and should have no trouble regaining your mastery of these practices.

Focused meditation is a major step toward the goal of stepping down the activity of your mind. It's crucial, therefore, that you have confidence in mantra practice before moving on to the next stages of practice.

Some people have challenges getting the hang of performing their mantras at a cadence and a volume that feels truly comfortable. This is mostly a matter of personal preference. However, if you find that you are saying a mantra at a level that is above a normal speaking voice, chances are that doing so will distract you rather than help you focus.

If you continue to have trouble with your mantra, try a simpler or more familiar one. Many familiar religious prayers are forms of mantra, particularly if they serve as a reference of comfort or a haven of security for the person reciting it. If reciting the Lord's Prayer is comfortable for you and you can do that without being distracted, by all means choose that or a similar prayer as your mantra. Remember, the mantra is there to command your focus in a way that makes it both comfortable and relatively effortless for you to repeat it without becoming bored or distracted. In addition, if you find your mind wandering as you are performing a mantra practice, you need to either look for another – possibly more basic – mantra or go back a few steps and lock in the foundational practices that lead up to this stage of instruction.

Chapter Seven
- Open Heart Surgery -

With your developing skills in non-focused and focused meditation, you have reached the point where you start looking inward in many truly exciting and spiritually promising ways. Though you may think of yourself as a novice, that's a relative term.

Dzongsar told me that after 80 years of practicing meditation he felt that he was just now "beginning to get somewhere." It was generally acknowledged around the monastery that he was in his mid 80s when I received instruction from him.

At some point over the past 24 days since you began this program, certain vaguely spiritual questions or notions may have occurred to you. This is to be expected, since when we remove mind-clouding distractions, other thoughts and ideas that have been pushed down deep begin to rise to the surface. All of us wonder about who and what we are at some point in our lives, though the hectic nature of our days often prevents us from thinking actively about these issues.

Several months after I first began to meditate, my mind was literally racing with questions about who I was and what I was doing here. I also began to question why I applied so much of my energy to business. In addition, even though I found that I was generally more tolerant of people, I was less willing to accept extremely selfish or non-compassionate behavior from them. I share this to reassure you that these feelings and questions are perfectly normal.

As I was learning meditation, I often observed the behavior of others. I found myself taking aside subordinates and asking them how they would have liked to have been on the receiving end of what they had just doled out to one of their staff or a customer. Other executives have told me that at the initial stages of meditation (within the first 60 to 90 days of practice) that they too have gone through periods of similar observation, questioning and change. Take it all in stride. And remember, it's not a race: Meditation is both a practice and a process of growth and enlightenment.

Chances are that when you engaged in the functional mindfulness practice in Chapter Three, your behaviors, thoughts and intentions were not always consistent with those that Mother Theresa might embrace. Executives don't get paid to "play nice." They do get paid to make tough decisions—decisions that sometimes result in people losing their jobs. They also get paid to keep costs down, resulting in tough talk to a vendor or veiled threats to an employee who isn't meeting his goals. The higher up you are on the corporate ladder, the more likely it is that being mindful of how you behave may not make you feel good about yourself.

As executives learn meditation and become mindful of the outcomes of their actions, some complain that they lose their "edge." One high level executive to whom I taught basic meditation called me one day and said, "I just don't *feel* like acting like a bastard anymore." When I inquired what the problem with that was, he responded, "But I have to be a bastard to do my job well!"

I understand this dilemma and empathize with people facing it. I've held several boards of director positions and the CEO title several times in my career. As you meditate and become more aware and sensitive to the impact you have on those around you, you'll find it virtually impossible to turn your back, shrug your shoulders and say, "Hey, business is business."

If you're practicing meditation seriously, "business is business" is quickly recognized for just what it is: a rationalization for people who are doing something they'd likely **not** want to see on the front page of the business section the next day. As a business professional charged with accomplishing complex and challenging agendas, how can you accommodate such a dichotomy?

The answer is balance. More specifically, you must balance the heightened awareness that meditation brings against difficult corporate objectives. How to achieve this balance is the single most frequent question I get from executives at breaks during the workshops, seminars and retreats I teach. The following example illustrates the concerns many executives have related to this balance issue.

Case study 7-1: A Moment of Truth

Don is a man in his mid 50s and a Vice President of Sales in a moderate-sized company. Don was under tremendous pressure to achieve ambitious financial goals. When I first met him and asked why he wanted to learn to meditate, Don said, "If our sales don't make budget our CEO only goes one place to take someone's head off. He is neither a patient nor tolerant man."

After first trying to convince Don to at least consider solving one aspect of his problem by changing where he worked, I began explaining some of the basic techniques that have been covered earlier in this book. Don encountered some difficulty in the Functional Mindfulness exercise and had to spend a bit more time on that than is the norm. After about six weeks of on-and-off teaching, I began to show Don the early instruction on reviewing the inventory created when performing Functional Mindfulness practices.

A few days later, Don called me in a very agitated and frustrated state. After a bit of probing, I learned that what had upset Don was his recognition that he tended to be very hard on people that worked for him. He was so incredibly focused on getting the job done that he was unaware of how he treated the people on his staff.

I tried to put his situation in perspective with anecdotes of some of the maliciously nasty bosses I had encountered — one in particular who boasted of having fired people while they were confined to the hospital — but Don's agitation increased.

Finally, I stopped the conversation and asked, "Don, just what is it that you're saying here?" To my genuine shock he replied, "I can't tolerate *myself* this way. If this is what's involved, then I need to find something else to do with my life." It's very difficult for me to convey the commitment in Don's voice at the time, but suffice it to say, he clearly sounded like a man that was going to make some changes. Becoming mindful was a tremendous awakening for this man.

I knew Don had a large family and a few college-age children, so I convinced him not to make a rash decision. Instead, I prompted him to go to the CEO of his company and in a very rational, calm tone explain that the pressure created by the CEO left him with little choice but to consider leaving the company. He also conveyed to the CEO that the current "tone" was so destructive that it was reducing sales, since the entire sales staff operated in a "hunkered down" posture almost all of the time. They were more fearful of doing something wrong than of performing up to their potential.

Probably half the CEOs in this country, presented with a similar scenario, would simply say, "Fine, there's the door." But in this case, the conversation with Don (in a fairly back-handed way) helped the CEO to become aware of what an irrational tyrant *he* was. He saw how unproductive his tactics were, not just in human terms but also in compromising the mental state of his entire sales staff, which in turn was costing the company sales.

The post mortem of this case is that Don still works at the same company. He's now within a few years of retirement and has become a committed and incredibly proficient meditator. In fact, he uses meditation to counterbalance the times the CEO slips into his old habits and begins to ratchet the pressure up to levels that compromise productivity. I mentioned to Don some time ago that he might consider suggesting meditation to his CEO, but he muttered that, being fairly close to vesting, he "didn't want to push it too far." It's actually a shame that Don didn't take advantage of the small battle he'd just won; who knows what that company might have accomplished had the CEO actually taken up meditation!

+ + +

As you learn meditation and your mind progressively relaxes, you will inevitably begin to reflect on who you are and how you conduct your daily affairs. As you do so, the chances are that you will feel compelled to be introspective at certain points. I have reached a few major points of introspection in my life as a result of meditation. All of them, without exception, have been tremendous growth experiences both personally and professionally.

When you find yourself at these introspective points, be open-minded and give yourself the time to explore who you are. Be prepared, though, to see yourself and your past conduct in ways that are contrary to the more idealistic picture that your ego might have painted.

In 1993 I went through such a period after practicing a form of hybrid meditation that I had stumbled upon by pure accident. The spiritual awareness and insights that ended up flowing through me were staggering. Virtually 90% of my life view shifted in a major way during this time. My priorities underwent a dramatic reshuffling. The clarity that arose in my awareness led me to pretty much leave the corporate world and pursue a life of compassion, teaching meditation and sharing what I have learned with others. For those that have an interest in learning more about that particular journey, the events are chronicled in my first book, *Beyond the Broken Gate*.

Few people ever undergo that level of dynamic life transformation. Still, you should be aware that such awakenings are not only possible but beneficial to your meditation practice. The more compassionate we become, the closer to our true state of origin we are. If we choose to call that "being closer to god," or any similar spiritual characterization, that's fine. To understand how this awakening will help you become more proficient at meditation, the following parable of logic and universal reality is useful:

♦ Whatever is occurring in our present lives is a direct product of our past behaviors and decisions. Here is a simple analogy illustrating this principle. If you receive a notice from the Department of Motor Vehicles that summarizes charges for a speeding ticket plus a posting of accrued penalties for not paying the ticket, it's fairly safe to assume that, at some point in your recent past, you probably have been speeding and failed to pay attention to the ticket. It certainly didn't arrive in your mailbox as a random event.

♦ If you take this DMV notice and simply toss it in the garbage, believing the system is incompetent or ineffective, would you feel vindicated if the following month you opened your mail and saw a larger fine added to the same ticket? Probably not.

♦ Next, you receive a message on your home answering machine from your insurance agent. They too have been notified by DMV of the infraction, and the rates you pay for your car insurance will be going up a bit.

♦ You take the second notice and also throw that one in the garbage. A few weeks later as you are once again speeding down the road, late for work, you get pulled over again. Now, you're not simply getting another ticket, you're getting a pair of handcuffs and a ride to the county jail.

There are two ways to respond to this hypothetical scenario. The first way is to say, "Oh, well, obviously what the person *should* have done is just paid the ticket when it came the first time." Certainly this course of action would have avoided all the headaches that ensued. The second way — the *mindful* way — is far more effective. What if this person had never been speeding in the first place? There would be no unfortunate chain of events if he had refrained from speeding.

How many situations in our lives would be far different — how often would we be far better off, in fact — if we never committed the initial triggering event? Much has been written about the amazingly effective Six Sigma approach in business and the empowering benefits derived by circumventing errors before they occur. Mindfulness practice is simply a personalized form of Six Sigma applied against the grid of how we go about our daily affairs. It affects everything from how we interact with our family members to how we treat those with whom we work; it even extends into the vast horizon of all that we do, say or think.

Stop for five minutes here and review the day that has just past. How could it have gone differently for you if you had been proactively mindful of your conduct and demeanor? What circumstances were you *responding* to as opposed to initiating? In short, how could you have changed what was your day this day, by applying the basic concept of ***not speeding,*** as a way to avoid having to deal with the "tickets" that pop up all day long in our lives?

Just how much aggravation was created and mental energy wasted in the speeding ticket scenario? How much less distracted would this individual have been had none of the post-speeding events occurred? All he needed to do was to be mindful of the potential outcomes of his actions as he was taking them: speeding in the first place; not paying the ticket the first time; ignoring the notice from the DMV; tempting fate by ignoring the second notice from the DMV; and being caught speeding again, which brought the entire series of events to their unfortunate conclusion.

Actions have consequences. To avoid unpleasant consequences, don't engage in actions that can trigger them.

Lesson Seven: Improving Relationships

Let's deal with the pragmatic elements of this incredibly powerful notion of ***not speeding*** for a moment. All of you who are reading this book are involved in very active and stressful lives. Chances are good that stopping or even slowing down daily to be mindful of each action and thought would not be practical.

What you *can* do is learn to look forward by looking back. In so doing, you accomplish many of the same objectives.

The "Open Heart" practice is about dramatically improving every aspect of business and personal relationships. Striving toward non-triggering behavior is improvement in ourselves. The goal is to achieve one improvement a day for five days.

I have never had anyone begin this practice who did not

extend it well into the future. They end up feeling so much better about themselves that extending the exercise further – and thus extending their personal growth — is irresistible. Just as importantly, people who apply this practice with true commitment find that they receive compliments from business associates and others about their new demeanor. The benefits are so wide ranging that trying to become even better each day is the natural response.

Exercise #7: Open Heart Practice

"Open heart" originates in the Twin Hearts Chakra meditation. The first element of the Twin Hearts practice requires that the person performing the mediation become intensely beneficent and embrace the world. For the Open Heart practice, we strive to accomplish this objective by improving the relationships we have with the people we know. We'll leave the rest of the world out of it for now.

This is the first exposure that you will have to performing a "mixed" practice. Open Heart practice is a combination of focused meditation followed by a brief period of overtly conscious introspection. Focused meditation is done first in order to open up the gates of the mind, so introspection will be more genuine and revealing.

♦ You will need your meditation journal with you and something to write with.

♦ Begin by performing the focused meditation practice detailed in Exercise Six, with the modification that you will now go directly into focused meditation without first performing the "Mindfulness of Breath" aspect of that exercise. In the Open Heart practice, perform focused meditation for 10 to 15 minutes as the initial element of the practice.

♦ Remember, concentrate on and seek to "enter into" your mantra. *Feel* the cadence and the inflection of the mantra's syllables. Without straining, try not to slip into repeating the mantra mindlessly or change the cadence of it to the point where it becomes meaningless to you. Think of a particular piece of music that genuinely moves you. At some point, the music seems to almost transport you someplace else because you have, in a way, implanted yourself within the music. It is almost as though you have temporarily "become" the music. Use your mantra in the same way.

♦ After 10 to 15 minutes of focused meditation, allow the following thought to enter your conscious mind: You are going to bring this portion of the meditation to a close for now. Imagine you have been driving on the freeway for a time. You see the sign for your exit and slowly take your foot off the gas. Do not hit the brakes…very gradually slow your pace. Most people accomplish this by steadily slowing down the repetition of their mantra.

♦ With this driving analogy as you guide, "signal" to yourself that you are making a definitive change at this point. Since you'll be getting off at the next exit, gently take your foot off of the gas and begin to lightly depress the brake. In much the same way, use your "turn signal" to remind yourself that you are making a change here. You can use any "prompt" that works, but I actually say to myself, "Slowing it down now." Allow yourself a minute or two to make a transition from "slow" to "stop."

♦ After you stop your focused meditation, open and close your eyes a few times. When I do this, I leave my eyes open a bit longer each time. When I am ready to leave them open, I remain in my meditating position for a couple of minutes. As odd as it may sound, the "signal" that I use to indicate that I have left the meditation mode and am back in my day-to-day environment is, "Not in Kansas anymore." You can create any affirmation you'd like, but I have found it helpful to have some definitive trigger that makes it clear that I'm no longer meditating.

♦ The balance of the Open Heart practice involves reflecting on what occurred during your most recent day. Even though you cannot always effectively practice mindfulness day-in and day-out, you can contemplate your actions from the day before. If you **had** been more mindful as you were proceeding throughout your day, what might you have done differently? What might have been easier if you'd made more mindful decisions or chose different actions? Is there anything you wouldn't have been forced to "clean up" after yourself at a later date? In short, looking at the past day, what might you have done that's similar to "not speeding."

♦ In your meditation journal, write down the top three events or interactions that, were you given a chance to go back in time, you would choose a different course of action.

♦ This is not an exercise in ethics or values or an exercise in self-criticism. Instead, the Open Heart practice is an opportunity to improve every relationship in your life by looking at what you did and what the outcomes were relative to other actions and better outcomes. Just remember the "no ticket" analogy and you'll have the idea. We're all familiar with that expression, "If I only had it to do all over again…" The object of the Open Heart practice is to prepare you for a similar situation. Having reflected on your previous actions, you'll be equipped to recognize when to take a different, more mindful path in new circumstances.

♦ Now, look at your three entries and ask yourself: What would it have been like to be on the receiving end of those actions?

Was there a way to have accomplished my objective in a more compassionate way? Was what I did (or how I reacted) even necessary? If a similar scenario arises tomorrow, how could I handle it differently?

♦ Open Heart practice should be performed twice a day for five straight days. Allotting 10 minutes to perform the retrospection should be adequate. Remember, this exercise won't work if you say, "Here's what I did wrong." Instead, look at it as, "Here's what I did, here's what happened because of it and here's how I can change how I do things."

♦ Discord in the workplace and in our personal lives creates enormous stress and anxiety. It also creates vicious cycles of "victim" and "victimizer"that lead to unproductive future outcomes. It compromises our relationships, the productivity of people up and down the line and our own effectiveness as business people. This doesn't mean that we all have to walk around with our hands folded emulating Mother Theresa, but we can strive for basic balance.

If you work diligently at the Open Heart practice, if you consistently review your own actions in terms of cause and effect, you will end up being a far better manager. Your business and personal relationships will improve by virtue of having increased your empathetic skills.

You'll also find that those relationships that define who we are and how we conduct our lives will be far more fulfilling. Your perception will become more acute, which in turn allows you to see problems from many different angles simultaneously. As those improvements unfold for you, every element of your life will begin to work better.

Troubleshooting

Some people have difficulty performing the Open Heart practice without becoming self-critical. That is a very natural reaction. Imagine the person in our speeding ticket vignette as they are being hauled off to jail. Chances are they're not complementing themselves on how brilliantly they handled the entire situation.

If you find that you are having difficulty selecting three events as you reflect on the cause-and-event actions of your most recent day, pick a fairly innocuous one to begin with. Look for things where in retrospect, you find yourself saying, "Now that was silly," as opposed to scenarios where you are saying, "I can't believe how incredibly stupid I am!" Start with smaller, less important events and work your way up.

Remember, the idea is to make more reflexively mindful actions the next time you face a similar scenario, not to flagellate yourself over what you did during these recent events.

If after trying this methodology you're still having difficulty, try performing 10 minutes of Mindfulness of Breath practice instead of the focused meditation practice. Then gently segue into the reflective segment of the Open Heart practice.

Chapter Eight
- Who's Asking? -

As you practice the lessons in this book, you may find yourself becoming more spiritually curious. This is a natural byproduct of quieting the mind through meditation. Such inquisitiveness is great, and the questions that arise can be directed toward an intense form of meditation.

We often complain that "my entire life is my work" because we simply don't allow ourselves the opportunity to balance the scales. I decided to include the "questioning meditation" – which I call the "Who's Asking?" practice – for those of you who aren't inclined to set aside 15 minutes twice a day for meditation (though you should realize that if you don't set aside the time, you won't get the full benefits of meditation). I've also included it because the "Who's Asking?" practice is tremendously useful for every meditator.

This is one of the more basic – and, in my experience, most profound – meditation practices existing. That includes some of the more complicated practices that take years to learn. It's powerful because it leads the mind into progressively deeper levels of intensity as it seeks to find an "answer" to just one simple question: "Who's asking the question about *who's asking*?" Or, as the teachers from the eastern traditions would say, how do we "know the knower?"

Who's Asking promises another value for those with extremely busy and unforgiving corporate schedules: It can be practiced almost anywhere at any time and under any circumstances. It is the only meditation that I use when I am waiting for the plane to depart. These days, that can sometimes equate to a very long meditation. On the other hand, if you have five minutes before a meeting and you feel that quieting the mind by just a little might be valuable, you can perform Who's Asking while sitting in the conference room.

A caution at this juncture is appropriate. Forgive the following aphorism, but it gets the point across: What appear to be the simplest things in life can often be made the most difficult. Just ask my brother-in-law who tried to teach me to hit a golf ball. Once every three years or so someone drags me out to the golf course. For the life of me, I cannot understand *how* the pros can swing so (seemingly) effortlessly and have the ball end up two feet from the hole! The Who's Asking meditation is very much like that. If you have the unfortunate experience of making it far more complicated than it is, you'll "get there" with the same kind of effortless swing that the pros use to drop the ball within inches of the target as soon as you "loosen your grip" and just allow it to happen.

Lesson Eight: Finding Heightened Awareness and Clarity

The Who's Asking practice is about trying to understand who and what we are. It is both a deeply spiritual and an incredibly pragmatic exercise. A variety of techniques can be applied to achieve the benefits of this brand of meditation. We'll limit the method used here so that you can perform Who's Asking literally anywhere and almost at any time you feel so inclined. Dzongsar once made me do this practice standing on my head for one minute to drive home just that point. "See, any monkey can do this even swinging from a tree," he added.

A significant percentage of the people who engage in this practice have found that, after a period of a week to several months, they feel as though they are sometimes operating in a euphoric cloud. I had this experience when the practice was first taught to me. Of course, being the kind of teacher that he was, Dzongsar immediately admonished me to "forget the experience and retain the lesson."

Who's Asking will lead most people to a state of mental acuity that true meditation experts call "heightened awareness," or what Dzongsar used to call "a place of significant clarity." If you achieve such a state and recognize it as extremely pleasant (as most do), by all means enjoy it. However, focus on remembering the meaningful insights that you had in the process of arriving at this feeling. That is what Dzongsar meant when he admonished me to "forget the experience and retain the lesson."

The Who's Asking practice can take you to states of introspective consciousness that are significantly different from your normal "grounded" state that helps you function. The state of introspective consciousness is probably different from anything that you have encountered before. Always allow yourself several minutes at least to return to your normal state of being after you practice this exercise (or any similar meditative practice that you perform, for that matter).

The first time I emerged from such a state under the instruction of Dzongsar, I insisted that I was "fine," but it took me close to three hours to make my way home. I only lived about 35 minutes away from the monastery, but I have no recollection at all where I spent the three hours. So be careful.

Periods of intense focus while meditating are not unlike focusing intently on a crucial work project. You pour so much energy into the process that you're left feeling drained and woozy afterwards.

Exercise Eight: Who's Asking

It is best when you are first learning Who's Asking to perform it where you normally meditate. As you become proficient, you can perform it almost anywhere at any time. A strong word of caution: Do *not* perform this meditation while driving. Ever.

As with all meditative practices, don't use it if you are extremely agitated or upset. Calm down before attempting it.

♦ As you start to learn Who's Asking, retire to your place of quiet and mindfully prepare the room in whatever way makes it most comfortable for you. Readying the room is such an important step because it serves as a kind of mental preparation – an advisory to the mind – that you are getting ready to meditate. After you have been doing this for a while, your mind will recognize these steps of preparation and begin to wind down on its own.

♦ Get comfortable, close your eyes and go through whatever initial practices you have found helpful to "signal" that you are beginning your meditation. Begin by performing the Mindfulness of Breath practice for about five minutes. You do not need the visualization portion of this exercise here. Just be mindful of each breath in and be mindful of each breath out. If you find some form of visualization helpful in performing this practice, though, do the following: As you breathe in, envision the air filling your lungs (I see it as a kind of idyllic Caribbean blue going in). As you breathe out, see the air flowing outward (I envision the red-orange smog color that used to hang over

Los Angeles when I lived there). Remember: Focus on being mindful of your breathing and nothing else.

♦ After approximately five minutes, use your "signals" to wind down the mindfulness part of this practice. Make yourself aware, however, that you will be going onto another practice. In my case, I acknowledge to myself that I am "moving on to Who's Asking now." Experiment with what works for you until you can "instruct" your mind that you are slowing down the Mindfulness of Breath practice but are not coming all the way out of your meditative state. This "instruction" also tells your mind to shift gears and begin the sequence that you will use to perform the Who's Asking meditation.

♦ Begin to focus on the back of your eyes (with them still closed, of course). It is crucial to perform this focus with true balance — neither too intently nor too casually. As I recall, Dazongsar initially explained this by telling me, "You will have found the correct balance in this part of the exercise when you are not cross-eyed yet also close to cross-eyed at the same time." Recognizing how frustrating an instruction that is, I should add that focusing on the back of one's eyes is a gentle and most definitely *not* uncomfortable feeling. If in your attempts to find this specific balance you feel ill at ease or nauseated, you are focusing too hard. Spend some time getting comfortable in just this portion of the exercise. Learn to hold your focus there and go no further until you feel ready.

♦ When ready, retain the focus on the back of your eyes and begin to ask yourself, "Who or what is it that is focusing?" There are several alternate forms of this question, any of which can be as effective. Which form of the question you choose to use is completely up to you. Here's a partial list of variations on the same question:

- Who's asking?
- Who am I?
- Who is it that is asking, "who's asking" this question?
- What am I?
- Who is the "knower" here (This is the one I use)?
- Who is it that is meditating now?
- What is this?

◆ Ask yourself the question repeatedly, but not nearly with the frequency or at an even cadence the way a mantra is used in focused meditation practice. I once asked Dzongsar how many times he actually repeated the question in a 30-minute course of performing this meditation, and his response was, "probably one time for every ten times that I inhale." Dzongsar told me that this exercise was similar in some ways to striking the gong and following the sound. Allow the question, "Who's asking the question?" to take you wherever it goes," Dazongsar said. "If you find yourself no longer engaged in considering the question, then it's time to ask it again," he added.

◆ Who's Asking should be practiced for five days straight, once in the morning and once in the evening. If it takes you longer to become comfortable performing it in your office, on the train, in a waiting room, etc., then continue to practice it in your normal meditation environment until you can do this practice easily. The goal is to be able to do the exercise without distraction in any venue.

Who's Asking — or any one of the numerous variations of it — is both a focused and a non-focused meditation practice that places it squarely in a meditation "no man's land." If you lead an inordinately busy life, though, it is a resource of mindfulness that you should call upon when needed.

If this practice catalyzes your desire for deeper experiences or explanations, contact a Buddhist, Hindu or other non-religiously affiliated meditation center. If your approach and determination to learn is serious, you will find the people at such centers more than willing to provide instruction and help you pursue insights. If you choose this route, please learn their customs, practices and be mindful of their sensitivities. For instance, the people at these meditation centers often don't care about assets and liabilities, unless you are referring to balance of your spiritual accounts.

For many business people, though, this practice is all they seek. It offers deep serenity, a respite from the demands placed on them during the course of a day.

Troubleshooting

The brilliance of the Who's Asking practice is its simplicity. Sometimes when people are learning this practice, they make it more difficult than it actually is. If you find yourself becoming frustrated while learning this practice, loosen your grip.

Although the results of this particular exercise can be intense, executing this form of meditation itself should not be difficult. Who's Asking is a practice of relaxation. The posture from which it is performed is one of ease. There should be no mental strain applied whatever.

You might encounter some early challenges during the changeover from the Mindfulness of Breath practice into Who's Asking. This is no different than sitting in a chair and deciding to go to a different room in the house. First, you need the volition to move and the understanding of where you will be going. Simply acknowledge your desire to gently shift from the Mindfulness of Breath exercise into the Who's Asking practice. When I do this meditation, I use the signal, "Now, where are the backs of my eyes?" to help direct me to exactly what I need to do next in order to start the sequence (and to get me in the questioning frame of mind).

Who's Asking is not a spiritual instruction. However, Who's Asking is a tremendously powerful meditation that often leads people to pursue greater insights into their spiritual practices. Therefore, do not become frustrated or resentful if, in the process of performing this practice, you entertain thoughts of buying another book on spirituality or pursue some other pathway of deeper insight. Likewise, if after practicing Who's Asking, you are not motivated to run off and sit on the highest mountain in the Himalayas, it doesn't mean that you're doing anything wrong.

Chapter Nine
- Finding Tranquility Base -

Thus far, you've received fundamental instruction in four meditation practices: Basic Mindfulness, Focused (Mantra) Practice, Open Heart Practice and the Who's Asking Practice. You could easily devote your life to studying any one of these meditation practices. Some of the more remarkable Eastern disciplines dedicate an entire lifetime to a single focused meditation. One in particular requires the practitioner to repeatedly ask the question, "What is it?"

Since it is unlikely that you will have the time to practice esoteric pursuits with such intensity, you now need to determine which practice – or combination of practices – are most effective for you personally. It is equally important to establish a pattern of practice that can be conveniently worked into your hectic schedule. "Pattern," in this case, does not involve the inflexibility that some might think the word implies. It simply means defining the practice or practices that you can integrate routinely into your life.

You need to find the rhythm for your practice that takes you to the most relaxed and highest functional state without becoming an intrusion on your schedule. Back in the mid-80s, when I first learned meditation, I took to calling this integration of customized practice, "Tranquility Base." As I write this, I can still hear Dzongsar laughing uproariously as I said that to him. You see, Dzongsar began to practice meditation when he was four. Tranquility to him was something entirely different, something almost unknowable to westerners.

Dzongsar found my term so funny because I assumed incorrectly that "tranquility" was a place that one reached. Executives deal in goals, objectives, budgets that are made or not made. Thus, when I inferred to Dzongsar that "making it" to some base of tranquility was my goal, he immediately corrected my misassumptions. To do so, Dzongsar looked straight at me with great serenity said, "Tranquility is what we are, not where we are going. When you meditate, you are only taking away what you placed in your own path. Meditation helps you to get back to where you always were to begin with. Stay with it, and I suspect you'll get there in another few lifetimes." With that, he stood up, patted me affectionately on shoulder and walked into the monastery, laughing gently.

You'll recall early on I emphasized that you shouldn't force meditation practice. This tenet becomes key as you begin the process of weaving meditation into your everyday schedule of activities. Meditation is often practiced prior to stressful or challenging periods because it creates a physiological as well as a mental state of relaxation without compromising overall attentiveness. In fact, it enhances it. Dzongsar called this "heightened awareness." As you increase your effectiveness you will enter this zone yourself.

A brief meditation — say 15 minutes or so — prior to beginning the business day can give you a tremendous edge in dealing with everything from tense customer interactions to finding creative solutions for tough problems. Meditating immediately after lunch or sometime in the afternoon to buffer against the next wave of the day's pressures is also a good idea. Be aware that mediation sometimes results in a desire for a brief nap. Therefore, choose a specific practice for an afternoon meditation that will avoid drowsiness; I'll help you understand how to make this choice later in the chapter.

Back when I was a corporate officer in a Fortune 100 company, I used to make notes in my day planner regarding my meditation practice. After several years of doing so, I realized certain times and situations were better than others to perform a practice. Here's a brief summary of three year's experience taken from those planners:

Mindfulness of Breath Practice: Every morning at the office before taking the first call. If I had to fly someplace that day, I performed this practice on the way to the airport (as long as someone else was driving).

Focused Meditation Practice: After lunch, before the first afternoon activity. The reason I ended up with this particular practice at this time of day was because I learned that the activity of repeating a mantra kept me at a level of attention where I was far less likely to doze off. I found that five to seven minutes of Focused Meditation practice at this time of day was energizing and didn't interfere with my schedule. If someone interrupted me and asked me what I was doing I usually responded with, "Oh, I was just thinking about how to reduce the severance packages for your category of staff." For some reason, they never asked again.

Open Heart Practice: Each evening after dinner and before my time with my family. Not that I was an ogre but engaging in the Open Heart practice at this time helped me wind down from the stresses of the day. Just as importantly, it afforded me time to reflect on the past day and boosted my energy so that I could brainstorm how I might improve the next one.

Who's Asking practice: I also learned to perform the Who's Asking practice at times when my opportunities were very limited (waiting for the plane to take off, sitting in a waiting room, etc.). It proved to be a very effective method for increasing my energy and gathering my concentration before a period where I needed to focus intently. The Who's Asking practice is a five-minute "cat nap" for the mind. If practiced properly, it can afford you a tremendous surge of mental and emotional energy at precisely those times when you most need it.

Whether you opt to apply these particular practices as I did or some other way is completely up to you. Some people find that there are certain practices that they just cannot seem to get the hang of, no matter how diligently they try. In the event you find yourself in this situation, do not attempt to force the method into your practice.

The best way to learn which meditation practice or practices work for you is through trial and error. Do not be ashamed or frustrated if some practices take you more time than others to master. Accept that your mind will lead you in its own way to the format and schedule that is right for you. To help you discover which practices work best for your style and schedule, use the following steps.

Lesson Nine: Accepting Simplicity

Getting comfortable and finding an effective meditation practice should not be complicated. In fact, some of you are probably already aware of which practice or practices work best for you. If you're not sure, though, don't worry, since a little experimentation will give you the answer.

I realize, however, that it's easy to fall into the complexity trap. When I was learning to fly a plane, Bill, my flight instructor, would tell me that I made things far more complicated than they really were. He'd bellow, "You've already learned to land the plane, why do you insist on acting like you need to learn it again?" Business people tend to fall into this same trap because their daily lives are complex. More so than ever before, they're faced with decisions where there are no right answers. Because of the information revolution, they're overwhelmed by data. The speed with which events unfold makes it challenging to keep up with all the new trends, events and technology breakthroughs. It's no wonder, therefore, that they reflexively look for complexity even when things are simple. Everything having to do with a plane, too, seems to suggest complexity to a novice.

Granted, learning to fly a plane and learning to mediate are two different things. An airplane will do exactly the same thing every time the controls are manipulated in an identical manner. Shift the stick to the right and you'll begin to bank right. In meditation, though, you can give the identical mantra instruction to two different people and they may end up applying it in completely different ways, experiencing totally different results. In fact, you can almost count on it.

The key to this lesson, then, is accepting that individuality is implicit in meditation practice. Learn to accept that it will require patience to find your individual comfort zone for practice. It's like golf. I absolutely guarantee you that Tiger Woods and I could both swing the same exact three iron and the results would be, well … let's say not similar. The identical principle applies in the practice of meditation.

Exercise Nine: Personalize Your Practice

I have found that people are naturally attracted to the meditation practice that is best for them. Thus, if you have felt drawn to one particular kind of practice versus another while working through the practices in this book, go with that instinct. You can always come back to one or more of the other practices at a later date.

However, if you've diligently performed all of the exercises detailed but find yourself having difficulty integrating them into your day, then you still need to find a happy medium between work and meditation. To achieve this goal, try the following:

♦ Start a new section in your meditation journal. Call it something like "Finding my comfort zone," clearly conveying the intention of this exercise.

♦ No one practice is more important than another, but let's start by focusing on the morning practice as our anchor. If you can establish a first-thing-in-the-morning meditation practice, finding the time and patience to work on the balance of the meditation schedule often takes care of itself. Since the aim is to continue your meditation practice for the rest of your life, take the time to figure out which form of practice works best for you. Begin by going through your normal morning routine for a few days, but remain mindful of where you could most effectively insert 12 to 15 minutes of meditation practice. Meditate at different time slots through different mornings and observe how intrusive and how effective the process of meditating was. Note the impact on your business day; were you more alert at work when you mediated right after waking up or when you meditated right before you left for the office?

♦ After you've figured when you'll be meditating (remember, it is always your decision to say "I don't want to do that this morning,") begin by trying each of these four meditations for five days each:

• Mindfulness of Breath Practice
• Basic Mindfulness Practice
• Focused (Mantra) Practice
• Open Heart Practice
• Who's Asking Practice

Throughout the course of this practice period, make brief journal entries about your energy levels, emotional perspective, alertness index and any other criteria that you feel are important. You will find that one or two practice formats are standout performers for you. When most executives go through this experimental phase and reread their journals, they typically note that one practice is more effective than the others. Some executives, for example, have told me that the Mindfulness of Breath practice created noticeably higher states of energy for them which they found very beneficial in starting out their days.

♦ If it's obvious which practice is best for you before you complete the entire list, feel free to adopt that meditation as your morning practice and call it your own. Just be sure to write brief notes in your meditation journal (I recommend four or five times a day at a minimum) so that the right practice clearly emerges. If you're trying Who's Asking and you see several notes in your journal like, "11:15 a.m., more tired than I was yesterday" you need to take heed of that and investigate a better option for you.

♦ Depending upon how you are feeling about your meditation practice, and how much time you want to make for meditation, consider experimenting with each of the practices during a midday meditation and an evening meditation. Most traditional meditation instruction suggests that one morning and one evening meditation is adequate and appropriate. But most meditation instructors have never had the joy of facing an agitated board of directors or a CEO with flames coming out of his ears at 2:15 in the afternoon. If you feel that twice a day meditation is giving you all that you need, feel free to stick with that plan. If, through experimentation, you find that a midday meditation energizes you, gives you an added edge in coping with your afternoon schedule or helps you be more mindful in the afternoon, by all means add it to your practice.

♦ Over this same period of time (or even longer if you prefer), keep records of any non-scheduled meditations you might engage in, and write down how they work for you. If you have a doctor's appointment, you might allow yourself 10 minutes in the waiting room to practice the Who's Asking meditation. Note that in your journal and observe if there are any ensuing feelings of greater relaxation or comfort later in the day. Also, do not hesitate to record something that did ***not*** work for you. If you tried the Open Heart practice and found it unsettling in the middle of the day, just learning that is a very important piece of information! Remember; this is trial and error and there are no mistakes.

There have been some novel variations of this method that people have shared with me. The following case studies illustrate two ways of experimenting with different meditation practices and assessing their effectiveness.

Case Study 9-1: Whatever Works, Do It!

After being taught a few basic meditation techniques (not by me but by a by a friend who was an accomplished practitioner), Sally was having difficulty deciding on the technique that worked best for her. This was apparently more a matter of self-confidence than anything else. Sally's instructor felt that she had demonstrated proficiency relative to what she had been shown. Sally, however, felt she should have been "feeling more" after she meditated.

Her instructor suggested that she experiment with a few different practices and keep a journal in order to see if she noted any changes in how she felt or thought. Sally reluctantly agreed.

Having come from a background in the sciences, Sally feared that because she was the subject of her experiment, she wouldn't be able to observe herself objectively. So she asked her husband and her administrative assistant to take note of her behavior during the next 20 days; she informed them that she would be experimenting with a few different meditation methods.

Both her husband and her administrative assistant noted a four-day stretch in the 20-day period when they found her to be "in far better spirits than normal." Her husband mentioned a number of improvements in their relationship, from communication to sex. During this same general time frame, Sally's administrative assistant commented on her "being in an amazingly much better mood than normal when she arrived in the morning." Sally also kept a journal and as it turned out, this four-day period coincided closely with the time span when she herself felt the best and most energized. She wrote that she "also felt much more fulfilled" over this period of time.

During her time of experimentation, Sally had actually switched from one meditation practice to another technique. She learned that the Mindfulness of Breath practice afforded her greater energy than she normally experienced, but she also learned that the Who's Asking practice produced sparks of creative energy.

Any good scientist could probably poke holes in this methodology. But in this case, all that really counts is the end result: Sally ended up adopting a mixed practice: Mindfulness of Breath in the morning, Who's Asking around mid day and Functional Mindfulness in the evening.

I don't advocate having others keep your journal for you (if it were me I'd worry about becoming overly conscious of my overt behavior) but what's important here is that Sally found a beneficial practice she could adapt to her life by enlisting the help of others to help her validate her experimentation.

Case Study 9-2: Please; Don't Promote Me

Helping Alan learn basic meditation skills presented me with an unusual challenge. Alan, an accomplished, confident automobile executive in his late thirties, had been the subjects of complimentary articles in the busienss press, and he had several thousand employees working under him.

Based on what I'd read and heard, my assumption was that Alan might have trouble with focus when it came to meditation. Taking people with that level of responsibility to a place where they can quiet their mind sufficiently isn't always easy. Operating in day-in and day-out overload mode can make shifting mental gears a daunting task. Not in this case though. Alan was a natural.

Alan's ability to slide into a place of basic meditative focus in a matter of seconds was almost spooky. In fact, for a while I considered the possibility that he had been meditating for some time and that he was coming to this small group as a practical joke. He breezed though every challenge like it wasn't even there. Even the Functional Mindfulness practice didn't seem to slow him down.

When it was time to discuss the process of finding the best ways to fit meditation practice into the daily routine, I figured Alan would be ten steps ahead of the other group members. Part of me assumed he'd already sorted out his practice on his own and wouldn't even show up. Surprisingly, he did attend all the sessions. We had gone through the early part of the assignment and the group had been experimenting with a couple of different methods over the previous week or so. We had reached the point where we were going to share experiences and possibly work through any obstacles that people might have run into.

As everyone in the group was getting comfortable that night, I noticed that Alan had an unusually unsettled look on his face. I purposely waited to call on him last, hoping that whatever might have been bothering him would have been answered while dealing with someone else's issues. When I called his name he almost jumped like he'd been hit with a cattle prod.

As it turned out, this powerhouse executive with literally billions of dollars in corporate responsibility, this man who had to make on-the-spot command decisions from morning until night, was having great difficulty making a decision on something as basic as which meditation practice he wanted to use.

Mind you, he'd had no difficulty figuring out how to do any of the practices. But as he tried one practice for a few days and then another and yet another, he couldn't make up his mind what worked and what didn't work best for him.

As it turned out, Alan had skipped the first and most essentail stage in the exercise: a basic quieting of the mind. He was miraculously able to perform Mindfulness practice without being mindful of what *he* actually *felt*.

It is easy, particularly in this day and age when managers are forced to do more with less at three times the speed, to be unaware of how we feel. This brilliant executive was so attuned to each development in the business world, to every nuance of any development in his plant and to every subtle issue within his family, that he never allowed room for one more bit of hyper-crucial information into his consciousness: How *he* felt.

In choosing the meditation practice or practices that you intend to adopt, don't forget that in order to succeed in this exercise – and in the challenge of life as well – that you must be aware of your own feelings, thoughts, desires and needs. You're not much good to yourself, your family and to those around you if you don't allow that little bit of data to compute. In fact, you're eventually going to sabotage yourself at work as well, since emotional intelligence and relationship-building have become critical competencies for just about every manager. If you don't know how you feel, you're going to have problems being empathetic and aware of how your style impacts others.

As for Alan? Well, eventually he mastered Mindfulness practice. And by "mastered" I mean that he became aware of what he had previously been unaware of. Tellingly, Alan refused the last two promotions that came his way in order to make time for his family and himself. I haven't spoken with him in years, but the last time I did he told me he didn't regret his decision for a "fraction of a second."

The only failure is a failure to learn from perceived failures.

The most common stumbling block when choosing a practice is assuming that the "answer" lies in one single practice technique. As noted earlier, many great Eastern masters immerse themselves in a single practice (or technique) for their entire lives.

In a like manner, don't be reluctant to change your practice if you feel that you're not getting what you need from it, or even if you just feel like trying something else. Remember, meditation is not a rigid exercise. Some people make the mistake of imposing a severe discipline on their meditation practice. There's a fairly simple guideline that you can always rely on:

> **There is no thought that is "wrong," no feeling that is "wrong" nor any place that you can "wander off" to in your meditation that is "wrong" either. The objective is not to control the experience but to *experience* the experience, whatever comes. The only true failure that can occur is a failure to learn from your experience and move forward on the basis of what you learned."**

In going through the process of finding what works for you in meditation, allow yourself free rein in your experimentation. Within that free reign, though, there is a responsibility to document your efforts in order to glean the most information possible and most effectively plan your daily practice.

Imagine that you are the CEO of a chemical company. You've assembled the best minds in the business and equipped a lab with every possible piece of scientific apparatus. No expense has been spared. No PhD on the entire planet worth their salt has gone untapped. The assignment of this special unit you've put together? To come up with a formula that will bring about happiness, peace of mind, increase energy, satisfaction and make all but the most impossible relationships work brilliantly.

Great effort is being applied in this lab. All available skill has been assembled. Your board demands constant reports. The shareholders call day and night, wanting updates on how the project is progressing. You look in frequently on your multi-billion dollar team of experts. They're working feverishly. Not even a fool could mistake from a distance that real science – true experimentation – is going on here.

Then one day there's a call from the lab. You rush down with the excitement that only an investor who has waited seemingly forever for his patience to pay off can have. There, standing amid the crowd of white-coated scientists, is a woman obviously aglow in happiness. In the exchange of a few words she assures you that she has reached a far greater state of happiness and satisfaction than her life heretofore had ever afforded her. Every objective of the experiment gets checked off as she relates the changes in her life that have occurred since she began taking the miracle formula.

You turn to the head scientist and shake his hand enthusiastically. "This is great, this is wonderful! Magnificent!" you exclaim, "When can we begin production? How long will it take until….?" The scientist looks at you quizzically. "Production?

Production? Why, you never said anything about production. We just kept experimenting down here. You never told us you wanted us to be able to reproduce all this." If they'd only kept a journal…

+ + +

Many executives are reluctant to keep a journal. To some, it evokes thoughts of what a shrink might suggest. But look at what's at stake here. There's a reason that scientists at Harvard Medical School and other prestigious institutions have begun intensive scientific investigations into what goes on in the human mind during meditation. One of the most prestigious magazines in the world recently showed pictures of Buddhist monks meditating inside of a MRI scanner at Harvard Medical School, the team of investigating physicians staring at the results on the screen with true awe. After you become a diligent meditator, you'll better understand the importance of documenting the effects of meditation.

With so much at stake – your happiness, peace of mind, effectiveness and success at work, possibly even your health – isn't it worth it to be able to produce a positive outcome through a meditation practice and then duplicate the experience?

Remember, no experiment can ever be a failure if it leads you closer to what will work.

Chapter Ten
- After Thoughts -

This is not the end.
This is not the beginning.
This is not the beginning of the end.
It is....
the end of the beginning.

- Anon.

Earlier, I stated that meditation without practice is completely without purpose. Having learned how to practice, you're now on the cusp of a potentially limitless, empowering opportunity. To continue or not to continue is your choice.

As an executive, you need to make crucial decisions all the time. Deciding whether to meditate is one of the most significant choices you can ever make. I say that not only as the author of this book but as an ex-Fortune 100 corporate officer, ex-CEO and board officer. If I could go back in my career knowing what I know now, I'd urge every executive on staff to at least try meditation. Even if I were successful in getting only half my team to take up the practice, the return on the investment would be staggering. What I'd have to worry most about is headhunters raiding my staff left and right.

It's not just about having greater peace of mind, being happier, enjoying far more productive relationships or even being able to hit a better nine iron. The greatest benefit of meditation is by far the least talked about…in our part of the world at least. Aside from the improved sense of well-being, the enhanced interpersonal skills and the medical benefits (such as lowered blood pressure), meditation usually brings about a unique form of productive introspection.

In some people, this introspection can produce outwardly mild results. If you are one of those unfortunate people that is prone to road rage, for example, meditation may reduce that to road *anger* over time. If you persist in your practice, eventually that anger will probably give way to a more benign self-questioning of sorts: "I wonder *why* that guy is driving like an idiot?"

Given a bit more time and a deeper commitment to practice, you may quite possibly end up ratcheting even those comments down a few degrees, perhaps to something like, "The way that guy's driving makes me wonder if he just got bad news — like someone he knows was in an accident." One of the reasons that meditation works so well is not just because it calms us. Over time, it brings our minds to a state where we naturally choose calm over aggravation. What actually happens if you follow the Graybar Method diligently is that you move toward a place that says, "I have zero interest in cleaning out the attic so, do I really want to put X or Y in there knowing I'll just have to go in and remove it later on?"

The result to a physicist would look something like this:

Less clutter = less stress = greater peace of mind = calmness = happiness = greater efficiency = less desire to have clutter. It goes on ad infinitum from there.

Now, before you fear that you're going to turn into Mother Theresa, let me share with you a simple reality of meditation: It takes time. Personal change, such as in learning to automatically respond to the reckless drivers of the world, can take 20 years or more of significant practice. It certainly did in my case. But along the way you will see and enjoy marked improvements that make the journey more than worthwhile.

There's something else you should understand. Meditation is not a form of mind control, but rather mind quieting. The "control" comes about only after our quieted mind is no longer distracted. Then our mind says to our conscious self something like "Maybe you need to make some changes."

The kind of changes I'm talking about are only going to take place if, after looking at your own thoughts, behaviors and actions, *you* decide to change them. Any changes that come about will be completely of your own volition. Meditation doesn't alter your life automatically — you have to do the work. You would be surprised, though, just how quickly people *do* decide to make changes not long after beginning meditation practice. Particularly Mindfulness practice.

Dzongsar used to say that once a person views his own behaviors and conduct from the perspective of an uncluttered mind, he runs to make changes like a man with his hair on fire. Then he would always comically add, "And those are the ones that are not fleet of foot!"

As I have explained this reality to people interested in exploring meditation over the years, Dzongar's answer to me has been my answer to them when they inevitably ask "Why? What is it about telling our chattering minds to 'shut up' for a few minutes that compels us to want to urgently change how we act?"

As you've already gathered from experimenting with the practices outlined in this book, meditation enables us to be far less distracted by the world around us. The "tape" that runs inside of us all day long — the one that pays attention and "writes down" absolutely everything we see, think, hear, say, do — begins to play back, albeit softly at first, as a kind of gentle reminder to us of what transpired that day.

The playback is fairly subtle initially. As we become more proficient in our techniques and reap the cumulative benefits of extended practice, there's less "noise" playing in the background as we replay the day's tape. Our perspective on the past day is in sharper focus for us than it used to be.

Several years ago I was explaining all of this to a friend of mine who had never meditated. With a look of total sincerity, she asked, "Then why do it? Why would I want to be reminded of all the things I said and did today that I'd rather *not* be reminded about?" I was hoping that it was a rhetorical question, but this woman actually needed an answer.

Your mind is like an incredibly amazing computer. The absolute power and marvel of the human mind is as close to limitless as anything we'll get to experience in our lifetimes. The thing is, it's a double-edged sword. As amazing as the mind is as a computing and rationalizing device, it's ten times as powerful as an instrument of memory.

Events and thoughts that don't even vaguely register in our conscious minds are on that tape. More importantly, there are things we subconsciously would prefer *not* to register on the tape. And I'm not just referring to the litany of events that we consciously wish we'd not said or done.

No doubt, you come home from work each day with frustrations, resentments, questions and quandarys. As a business professional, your mind is overrun with more stressful and perplexing situations than you could ever record.

One of the primary reasons that I decided to write this book is my almost 30 years of being a corporate executive. I have seen few instructors of meditation who possess the experience, compassion and empathy required to ponder (much less truly comprehend) the unique pressures and life circumstances that corporate managers have to deal with every day.

The ethical/moral line of appropriateness when weighed against the interests of shareholders can become blurred. There are days when I suspect that every person reading this book wishes that he might borrow the wisdom of Solomon for just a few precious moments.

In the business world today, managers are sometimes forced to retain staff that they know are not competent, release employees that they know to *be* competent and make decisions that are often billed as "for the good of the corporation." And that's before the first coffee break. Executives' days quite often go downhill from there.

As intelligent beings, we use our brains to rationalize these activities. Since most executives are actually pretty smart people, we usually "rationalize" our way out of things pretty well. The problem is that our subconscious mind remembers all of it. We can repeat to ourselves over and over again, "It was really best for the business" — a rationalizer's mantra of sorts. Yet on the "tape" in our subconscious mind, those events are being played back inside our heads as, "Was I a son of a bitch today or what?"

When one adds enough "entries" like that onto our perpetually playing tape, it is very difficult – if not impossible – to feel very good about ourselves. The rational mind eventually loses out because it is only capable of supporting us while we are *actively* thinking about what we said or did.

In this case, when we stop the mantra, "It really was best for the corporation," the tape of the subconscious mind takes over and the results are almost inevitable; the subconscious mind starts affirming, "you are absolutely right, you *were* a son of a bitch today…and you were worse yesterday. You think you can pull that rationalization crap on me… ME? Who do you think you're kidding?"

And the subconscious mind never shuts up. It is the shrew of the universe and our choice is either to tame it or suffer its ceaseless condemnation of our actual behavior. In order to tame the shrew, we need to take away what causes it to shriek at us. The subconscious is a fairly honest creature; if we don't act like a son-of-a-bitch today it really won't complain that much. As we temper our behavior, the subconscious backs off a bit and, we end up feeling a bit better because there's not a voice constantly calling us unpleasant names. Of *course* we start to feel better about ourselves.

The explanation I gave my friend who asked, "Why do it?" so many years ago was a bit more extended, but she got the point. She was one of those corporate people who was all too consciously aware that she *had* to be a bastard to get her job done (in her mind at least). She viewed meditation as a mechanism of sheer compensation. She fell into the category of "meditate or medicate?" Medication — even the kind that comes in a fancy bottle slung by a bartender — is another choice often made by those in the executive ranks, under the illusion that it is actually solving problems.

Medication works by temporarily anesthetizing the subconscious for a few hours. ***Meditation*** addresses the cause and removes the subconscious' reason for speaking so rudely to us. At the same time, it gives our minds time to rest, allowing us to perform better; we become more compassionate and understanding in our jobs, our relationships (of every kind) and to ourselves. This results in even less cause for criticism and before you know if, the attic is clean and the shrew is tamed. And you thought Shakespeare was talking about a hypothetical character!

Meditation is better.

You made a choice to somehow come into possession of this book. That can only be a sign of recognition that there is some need in you, that you have too much of something (stress, noise, pressure, aggravation, unhappy relationships at home, at work, whatever) or too little of something (job satisfaction, a sense of making a contribution through your work skills, satisfactory relationships, peace of mind, a feeling of general well-being, joy, a degree of spiritual insight and security).

If you've read this far, you have some choices, and choices

are almost always good things. One of the choices is to get some relief from your dissatisfaction and frustration by changing some aspects of your life. More and more, as I have the honor of speaking to audiences around the country, I hear from executives who are contemplating meaningful life changes to address their problems. But you needn't quit your job to find the freedom from stress and the fulfillment from work that you seek.

The brilliant manager, Alan, cited in Chapter Nine who simply said, "No thanks," to a couple of promotions offers an example of the alternatives open to you. There are many similar "partial solutions" being created in the corporate environment today. You might find some of the insights noted in Appendix 2 to be of some value in that regard. These ideas and concepts are extracts taken from a speech that I share with corporate executives who want to modify their stress levels, enhance the way they feel about themselves and potentially explore learning meditation to cope with the rigors of corporate life. Since just walking off the job is rarely an option (although often a fantasy), my approach is to modify the factors that can be adjusted and provide mechanisms for coping with the challenges that remain. Meditation and modification of certain patterns are by far the most effective mechanisms of coping that I've found.

If you choose to become fully engaged in the meditation practices described in this book. I strongly suggest that you do *not* choose to do so in a half-hearted way. Meditation often has a subtle, sometimes even delayed, benefit. If your heart isn't in it, your soul and mind cannot possibly benefit from it. On the other hand, I promise you that if you dedicate your heart with sincerity to the program as it is laid out in the book and perform the practices with diligence, you – and everyone in your life – will be grateful that you made the effort. Within six months most people that take up and stay with meditation have others in their life asking them how they made such positive "changes."

One last note in this regard: If you feel that you need guidance or instruction in your meditation practice, never hesitate to seek it. Our web address is listed in the back of this book and we conduct several different levels of meditation workshops and seminars across the country. There are many other excellent instructors that you can reach out to, depending upon what discipline interests you or what kind of challenge you are having. Never be ashamed to ask for help. Had I not done so almost 20 years ago, I most certainly wouldn't be writing this book.

You can, of course, choose to do nothing. That equates to a resounding vote for the status quo, or a tacit suggestion to yourself that "everything's just fine with me…no problems…no worries." If you actually believe that, I suggest that you return for one last attempt at Exercise One. Observe the ceaseless activity in your own mind and ask yourself one simple question:

> At this point would I rather subject myself to the unrelenting commotion with which the world assaults me or would I rather seek out – even if just for a brief period during each day – the calm amid the chaos that meditation potentially promises?

I'd also like you to consider this: The week before he died in 1986, I found Dzongsar sitting in his favorite spot next to the rock garden. I suspected that he chose that place because it allowed him easy access to the stick he used to strike the gong and, more often than not, his most remedial student (me). But he told me that day that he simply liked the view from there.

It occurred to me just then how complicated we make our own lives. We open the credit card bill, look at the amount due and exclaim with mystifying sincerity, "How did it get that high?" As executives, nightmares land on our desks seemingly on a non-stop basis; how many of those problems, in realty, can we really deny all responsibility for? If you're looking for the engineer and architect of your issues and challenges in this life, most of the time you need look no further than the nearest mirror.

I pondered these issues on that summer afternoon as I watched Dzongsar staring placidly into his garden. I also considered that he was genuinely satisfied to watch over his rock garden just to observe the sunrise each day. Then there was me, trying to figure out how to buy the next more expensive sports car, the luxury house with more rooms than I would ever go into and anything else that required the sixth dimensional stretching of my paycheck. "Simple pleasures" was all Dzongsar ever said when I asked him about how he managed with so little.

I never had a clue that Dzongsar was ill. He could have been 20 years older or younger than he looked. On what turned out to be the last day that I spoke with him, he was as serene and calm as ever. He spoke to me as he always did, without judgment. If he felt anger or resentment over being ill, he never expressed it in any way. He never exhibited even a hint of arrogance, despite the fact that he had forgotten more than I would ever know about all things spiritual.

He was never shaken – if he knew he was dying you wouldn't have known it by looking in his eyes or listening to his voice. He said many things to me on that particular day, but none as profound or as lasting as this:

> All that you will ever want or need lies within the quiet that resides inside the silence of what you think of as you. Whenever you perceive that you have found that place of silence, look just one shade deeper. That one shade deeper is the journey that holds the promise of total inner peace and happiness.

I'm still looking. Twenty years have passed and so far, I have found incredible inner peace, happiness, poise, enhanced productivity in my work, better relationships than I ever believed I could manage and balance. My income is far greater than it ever would have been had I remained on the course I had been following before I began to meditate. If I have any fears, including death, I am unaware of them.

Just like everyone else though, I do have bad days. I have times when I don't particularly *feel* in balance or at peace. Life is by no means perfect, but then again, as Dzongsar always reminded me, life is a constant work in progress made either more or less tolerable through quieting the mind. He's right. That much I can swear to.

I have yet to unravel the mystery that Dzongsar left for me that day. I probably never will. But of the little that I have absolute confidence in at this juncture of my life, I know that through the gift of meditation Dzongsar shared with me, I have all that I could ever want in this life. I also have the meditative tools that will support me wherever I might choose to go — in business, in my personal life and in my spiritual practice as an inquiring, card-carrying citizen of the universe.

My greatest hope is that, in your effort to find reduced stress, inner peace, true happiness (as opposed to the brand of transient happiness that comes from "things" and then evaporates as we grow bored with those things), stability and greater effectiveness in anything you choose to do, you too will accept the simple gift that Dzongsar shared with me. May happiness and profound peace be yours. As Dzongsar used to say, "Anything else that comes to us in life is just a gift atop another gift."

Appendix One
Practice Summary

The summary below is designed as a reference for your practice enhancement. It is not a substitute for reading the chapters themselves and thinking your way through the exercises in each chapter. There are no shortcuts to learning meditation.

If you find yourself stuck or frustrated with some element of the pathway outlined in this book, go back and re-read the chapter where you encountered difficulty and pay particular attention to the troubleshooting section in that chapter.

As noted in the early chapters of this book, each stage of this program is designed to use the technique and explanations in earlier chapters as foundation. If you're experiencing real difficulty in some specific exercise it may also be helpful to revisit the exercise in the immediately preceding chapter in order to assure that the foundation element established in that part of the program is firmly established

If after following those procedures you are still experiencing challenges my suggestion is to attend a meditation workshop or seminar. There is absolutely nothing to be ashamed about in this. I learned from a teacher after first experiencing unsatisfactory results by trying to learn through reference books. Back in the mid 1980s though, there were precious few books available and even fewer teachers offering organized courses.

Exercise One:

Objective: Recognition of the over-active "normal" state of our mind pre-meditative practices.

Method: Close your eyes and try to clear your mind completely (note, do not get frustrated if you have difficulty clearing your mind; this is the entire purpose of this exercise.) Just do the best you can to gently quiet your mind to clear it of all thoughts and forget all things currently occupying your mind. Allow your mind to go wherever it wants to or wherever it goes of its own momentum.

Observe and take mental note of what comes into your thoughts. Do this without judgment or criticism. You are *not* failing at your first attempt in meditation if you have difficulty focusing your mind. Your job is to observe what comes into your thoughts and simply note it.

Write down as many of the thoughts, ideas, feelings and anything you experienced during this period. These are the initial entries in your meditation journal.

Exercise Two:

Objective: Establish initial proficiency in the practice of "mindfulness." Mindfulness is merely a process of becoming consciously aware of what you are doing or even thinking. The difference is, mindfulness brings the awareness from the subconscious mind into the conscious mind thus creating a distraction as a product of the mindfulness focus.

Method: Begin by thinking about the most peaceful and restful state or place that you are capable of recalling. Whatever event or scenario affected you deeply from a positive perspective, think through each detail meticulously. Recollect the way you felt then and allow yourself to *feel* that again now.

As you bask in that feeling, take in a slow, deliberate, deep breath. As you breathe in, imagine that you enhance your ability to relive that place – that experience – with even greater clarity. Be aware that as you breathe in, the vividness of the imagery and each detail of the entire scenario as it originally occurred, increases. Now, slowly let that breath go and be aware of the fact that you are exhaling. As you exhale, *feel* yourself doing so. As unusual as it might sound, as you exhale say to yourself, "now I am mindful that I am exhaling."

Take another slow, deliberate breath in and as you do so, become conscious that you are inhaling. Feel the air going slowly into your lungs. As you breathe in though, be aware that you are doing so and say to yourself, "now I am mindful that I am breathing in." The cadence of your breathing cycle must be your normal respiration cycle or slightly slower. If you find yourself hyperventilating, stop, rest for a few minutes and start over with normal cadence in mind.

Continue this pattern for 10 minutes or so. The objective is to focus on the breath. Feel – and be aware of – the fact that you are breathing. You need accomplish no more in this particular exercise than to become aware of the very fact that you *are* inhaling and exhaling in a normal pattern and at a very comfortable pace.

Exercise Three:

Objective: Practicing functional mindfulness is designed to bring to our attention the kinds of thoughts, actions and intentions that we manifest as we go about our normal daily course of activities. By becoming aware of those actions and thoughts, we may decide on our own that we'd be better off without some of them or, possibly modifying some of our rougher edges.

Method: This exercise requires that you keep a journal for the period that you practice functional mindfulness. The headings on this part of the journal are simple: "Time." "I am mindful that:" and "Source:" In this case "Source" is the column where you will make a notation of *how* the mindfulness came to your attention – how it came about. Were you saying this to someone, thinking it, feeling it or even fantasizing about it?

What is most crucial is that you make the strident effort to actually *be* mindful during this exercise. The idea is to become aware of what you're doing and thinking while you're doing it and make even a very brief entry about it. Many people are surprised when they perform this exercise and as a result become aware of what they are doing and thinking all day long.

Exercise Four:

Objective: This is an exercise in reviewing and understanding the mindfulness journal. The journal's purpose is as a tool to help you look at what behavior patterns or other activities, including thought patterns, that you might want to eliminate or change in some way that *you* decide would result in a better, more peaceful and happier life for you and those people in your life that are important to you.

Method: Try to pick out the top three or four items in your journal that, to your mind, probably brought about an event or feelings of discord in you or even those around you. What you're looking for is entries that, when viewed objectively, obviously ended up with people being uneasy or even outright angry. That includes you.

Study each event or thought that occurred and visualize what the ensuing chain of events was that ultimately led to discord in your life. [I hung up on my spouse and I ended up sleeping on the couch as one example.] As you become mindful of those, see if you can raise your awareness of those actions or behaviors going forward such that you reduce or eliminate them from how you operate.

Exercise Five:

Objective: Periodic assessment in meditation is a valuable tool to help plot the course onward. This exercise is designed to assess progress to date by revisiting the monkey mind as outlined in Exercise One.

Method: Make a note of your "start time" in repeating the monkey mind exercise as you did at the end of Chapter One. Close your eyes and try to clear your mind completely. Allow your mind to go wherever it wants to or goes of its own momentum. Observe and take mental note of what comes into your thoughts.

The objective here is to observe what comes into your thoughts and simply note it. Look at the clock; write down the "end time" of this second monkey mind observation session.

In your meditation journal write down as many of the thoughts, ideas, feelings, anything you experienced — and whatever came into your mind — during this period as you attempted to quiet your thoughts.

Compare the outcomes in this exercise with the observations about the activity of your mind when you performed this exercise nine days ago. What differences were notable when you tried to quiet your mind this time when compared to the first time you performed this exercise? Did different subject matter come to mind? Were you more aware of the thoughts coming into your mind? What differences were there in your ability to pass the time without becoming frustrated or "frigidity" this time as opposed to last time? Was it easier for you to begin the actual process of trying to quiet your mind when you did the exercise this time as opposed to the first time?

Exercise Six:

Objective: This is an initial exercise in focused meditation. The purpose of focused meditation is to actively engage your mind on some specific item. Concurrent with that focus, the second objective of this technique is to allow your mind to take an ostensible deep sigh and relax. The two seem contrary to each other but they're not.

Method: Focused meditation often has better results if you create some form of formal self-acknowledgment that this is a time that you have chosen to meditate. Without affecting any specific practice elements, allow yourself to become aware of the surroundings.

Begin this exercise by performing the mindfulness of breath practice. Your sole focus at this point will be on your becoming mindful of breathing in and your mindfulness that you are breathing out. You must focus solely on the breath and, the cadence of your breathing. The essential part of this is to reach the deep recognition that it is *you* that is breathing. Your awareness of that breath is an awareness of yourself. Your objective is to practice this variation of mindfulness of breath for about five minutes.

Next make a subtle transition from performing the mindfulness of breath practice into effecting your mantra. When you begin your mantra it is best to start out slowly and work upwards to a cadence and pace that is comfortable for you. You will have achieved the best possible balance in repeating your mantra when you are aware of every syllable without being aware of having to *recollect* every syllable. What is most crucial in this practice is to achieve a state where the only "activity" any part of your conscious mind is engaged in is performing the mantra and being mindful that you are performing the mantra.

Focused meditation under this method of meditation should be practiced for 15 minutes, twice a day for the next two weeks (14 practice) days as it is the essential practice in this method and, the first stage where you will be integrating one practice form into another.

Exercise Seven:

Objective: The "Open Heart" practice is about dramatically improving every aspect of every one of our relationships by striving to effect non-triggering behavior improvement in ourselves.

Method: Begin by performing the focused meditation practice detailed in Exercise Six but modify the exercise by going directly into focused meditation without first performing the mindfulness of breath aspect of that exercise. In the open heart practice, it is best if you perform focused meditation for 10 to 15 minutes as the initial element of the practice.

Concentrate and seek to "enter into" your mantra. *Feel* the cadence and the inflection within the syllables of it. Without straining, try not to slip into repeating the mantra mindlessly or change the cadence of it to the point where it becomes meaningless to you.

After 10 to 15 minutes of focused meditation, allow the thought to enter. Most people accomplish this very effectively simply by slowing down the pace of their mantra. It's best after focused meditation to open and close your eyes a few times after you cease the process of active meditation.

The balance of the open heart practice involves a personal retrospective view on what occurred during your most recent day. Ask yourself; if I *had* been more mindful as I was proceeding throughout the day, what events might I have done differently such that I might have had easier to deal with results of certain actions or decisions?

Most critical for you to grasp in this regard is that this is not an exercise in ethics or values. Neither is it an exercise in self-criticism. The open heart practice is an opportunity to *improve* every relationship in your life by virtue of the process of looking at what you did and what the outcomes were as a result relative to how you might have acted in a way that would have had a better outcome.

Exercise Eight:

Objective: The *who's asking* practice is about beginning to understand the nature of what we are. It is at the same time both a deeply spiritual and an incredibly pragmatic exercise. The *who's asking* practice, if effected properly, will lead most people to a state of mental acuity that true meditation experts call, "heightened awareness" or what Dzongsar used to call "a place of significant clarity."

Method: Go through whatever initial practices you have found helpful to "signal" that you are beginning your meditation and begin by performing the mindfulness of breath practice for about five minutes.

After approximately five minutes has passed, use your "signals" to bring about the self-awareness that you will be winding down the mindfulness part of this practice but also make yourself aware that you will be going on to another practice.

Begin to focus on the back of your eyes (with them still closed of course). It is crucial to perform this focus with true balance – neither too intently nor too casually. The balance is best if you can focus on the back of your eyes so it is a fairly gentle and most definitely *not* discomforting feeling. If in your attempts to find this specific balance you feel ill at ease or nauseated, you are focusing too hard. Learn to hold yourself there and no further.

While retaining the focus on the back of your eyes begin to ask yourself, "Who is it that is focusing?" Here's a partial list of other, common iterations of that same question: who's asking? Who am I? Who's asking this question? What am I? Who is the "knower" here? Who is it that is meditating now? What is this?

This question is asked repeatedly but not nearly with the frequency or at an even cadence the way a mantra is used in focused meditation practice. There is no "right" or "wrong" process that can be applied in this portion of the exercise.

Exercise Nine:

Objective: The key to this lesson is adapting the various practices of meditation such that they comport with your individuality. The exercises that preceded this chapter are essentially tools in the toolbox. This exercise is figuring out which of those tools – or combination of those tools – will work best on the challenge of quieting your individual mind.

Method: This exercise requires dedicated journaling. Even though no one practice is more important than another, set an objective of securing the morning practice as your anchor. After you've figured when you'll be meditating begin by trying each of these five meditations for five days each.

- Mindfulness of Breath Practice
- Basic Mindfulness Practice
- Focused (Mantra) Practice
- Open Heart Practice
- Who's Asking Practice

Several times throughout the course of the days that you are experimenting with the various practice techniques it is crucial that you make brief journal entries about how you feel from; an energy standpoint, an emotional perspective, an alertness index and any other criteria that you feel are important.

If at any point in the course of trying out practice techniques it becomes very obvious to you that one practice is far more effective for you than another feel free to adopt that practice as your morning practice and call it your own.

You should go through the identical exercises for a mid day meditation and an evening meditation. Most traditional meditation instruction suggests that one morning and one evening meditation is adequate and appropriate. If, as a product of experimentation you find that a mid-day meditation adds incremental benefit (as documented in the journal that you keep), by all means add it to your schedule. If not and/or your schedule won't accommodate a short mid-day meditation, don't worry about it, twice a day will do.

General Info

Don't:

♦ Ever force yourself to meditate.

♦ Censor or criticize your thoughts or feelings.

♦ Shove an "issue" to the side; if you note some subject consistently arising in your mind, deal with it either on your own or if need be, by finding a professional to discuss it with. If it's coming up repeatedly, it's a sure sign that it warrants attention no matter what it is.

♦ "Dictate" how the meditation experience will unfold. Leave your expertise in controlling things at the office. Meditation goes where it goes. Let it.

♦ Get frustrated if you fall asleep. Even Dzongsar fell asleep sometimes. It's not a sign of failure, only of being tired.

Do:

♦ Make a commitment to the practice. I've purposely not noted any arbitrary time obligations that you should commit to because meditation is a totally individual experience. Some people note benefit after one session, others have spent months before noting even subtle changes. Just because you might not feel the changes doesn't mean they aren't occurring. Stay with it.

♦ Keep a journal. Only by so doing will you be able to recognize just how far you have come in your own eyes as time progresses. A journal can also be invaluable as a point of reference if you seek out a teacher.

♦ Feel free to experiment a bit once you have gone through the book and all of the exercises. Some of the most remarkable experiences that I've had from meditating trace their way back to my own experimentation with various methods and individualizing those efforts.

♦ Feel comfortable in seeking out workshops, teachers and other sources of information to improve your meditation practice.

Appendix Two
Seven Steps To Integrating Calm
Into Your Professional Life

Inevitably when I have an opportunity to talk with management-level people about their frustrations in life and what gives them the most trouble, they talk about two things; the feeling that the world is coming at them literally without as much as a three second break and, their dissatisfaction with the environment at work.

Hopefully, the exercises in meditation described in this book will afford you some degree of relief from the seeming ceaseless onslaught of the world. In speaking to groups around the country about the other issues that plague management, the general feeling of "things being out of control at work" sometimes has been knocked down a peg or two on manager's scales by keeping the following insights in mind.

It is crucial that you understand that, one of the reasons that we all suffer these kinds of frustrations is that we are most often both the architect and engineer of the very problems that we complain about the most. Traced back to their true origin, most issues that create the greatest difficulty for us trace their roots right back to our own doorsteps.

That being the case, to affect the greatest degree of "repair" to the issues, often the change must start with us and ultimately spread outwardly to others. This is all the more true if you are in corporate management and, exponentially more true relative to the 'altitude" you command on the corporate ladder. At a minimum though, you will find that by making some subtle changes in yourself (such as those you probably experienced when you performed the *Functional Mindfulness* practice) that many issues tend to be ameliorated or, even disappear.

Just envision some of the more noteworthy corporations that recently made it – albeit with dubious distinction – into the headlines. Would those headlines have read the same had management at the highest levels been demonstrating greater levels of ethicality and imparting those values down through the chain? Most certainly those problems didn't begin at lower levels and work their way ***up*** through the hierarchy of the executive suite. So here's your opportunity as a leader to put a stake in the ground for your employer and, yourself in terms of potentially improving your professional life in a number of ways.

(1) **Take the time to recognize what you are doing**. Every time you go against what you know, deep down, are universal spiritual principles – by failing to treat people with basic human decency – you do damage not only to your own soul but in fact, create a new 'distraction" for your mind to process. Your conscious mind might block out that you're acting like a jerk; the subconscious mind tosses that behavior straight up into the "attic."

Even for the hard-core business elite that takes the approach, "spirituality is for Sunday, business is business," the reality is that when you treat someone poorly in business or in your personal life it always comes back at you. If you're in sales and you ignore or just fail to service a customer you know what the result will be eventually. The reality of the world is that every time you take a short cut by running over someone or maybe even slicing the edge off of the ethics line, you're sending a message to others that this is how your corporate culture is defined and, you're subconsciously programming your own mind to remind you of what you did later on. That goes from treating an employee with disrespect to allowing an over-charge go through the billing system. If you do that, how long might it be before a subordinate is emulating that behavior? How long before your own mind has to deal with that clutter that *you* created?

Think long-term. You need not be a pillar of spiritual behavior in your day-to-day business affairs but if you're in management, be prepared that your behavior and values will be reflected outwardly through employees someday. Recognize what you are doing and what messages you are sending by your actions. Your behavior is a valuable long-term asset of the company. Treat it as such.

(2) Get in touch with your own values. Sometimes the cacophony of our daily lives makes it difficult to hear the music of our own souls – the place that we get our own unique "operating instructions" and values. When your boss or a major customer is screaming at you that they need something cheaper, faster and better it can be very hard to hear that music. Shortcuts beckon and tempt us at such times. It is at such times then, that you have to really pay attention to know what your own value system is.

There is real exposure in allowing your company's value system to replace your own. Meditate. Explore. Read some books on spirituality. Often in opening your mind you'll find that your own value system is generally very well grounded. Remember also, you got and manage to retain – the job you have because of the intelligent decisions that you make. That includes value judgment calls. Stay true to yourself and you'll serve your company at the same time.

And again, think long-term in determining what your values really are – bending the rules to get a bigger house or a nicer car is being a short-term investor. Besides that, you may have noticed that it's earned some people the wrong kind of stripes and an extended vacation in the prison system of late.

(3) **Devise a plan for determining what's o.k. — and what's not**. This always seems simple enough…right up until the point where we need to balance out our potential income against an issue that taunts the grey scale line. Back when I was still consulting to boards of directors on strategic issues, I once asked a CEO that found himself in a very tough position where pushing the ethics line a bit would have created a viable solution, to ask himself "what would Jesus do in this situation?" (He had already shared with me that he was a deeply "born again" believer.)

The CEO looked me straight in the eye and said, "Jesus didn't have my frigging balance sheet!" Despite my admonitions not to press his luck this CEO made a spiritually-questionable call and did something very un-Jesus like although it may well have allowed this business to survive for a while longer. Sometimes then, we need to adopt a more modern, pragmatic set of guidelines in figuring out what's o.k. and what's not. After almost 30 years in business, I've found this brief checklist will keep all but the most daring out of the deep water.

♦ Don't do anything that you wouldn't want replayed in living color for a group consisting of your best friends, your spouse and your mother.

♦ Begin and end every exchange with a co-worker, boss and particularly a customer by asking yourself silently "How would I feel if I were them in this exchange?" or "Would I feel treated fairly if this situation were exactly reversed?"

♦ Ask yourself, "How would I feel if what I am about to do was reported on the front page of the *Wall Street Journal*? This is the true platinum standard for business people. You'd be surprised how many people would be willing to face God, their spouse, their mother or the devil himself but wouldn't ever want to tolerate the embarrassment of the entire business world knowing what they did. Worthy of note here, the *Wall Street Journal* doesn't care about any rationalizing you might engage in. Therefore, when using this standard to check yourself, I suggest you apply the objectivity of a reporter to your evaluation.

(4) Determine if your workplace is out of sync with your value system. This is a complicated affair by any standard. Sometimes, as people adopt the practice of meditation and begin a process of introspection and, looking at what is really going on around them during the course of their day, they conclude that the culture of where they work is not exactly consistent with the style they're comfortable integrating into their life. The conflict here, of course, is that good jobs are difficult to find. And leaving the one you have can be a tortuous process.

Over the years I have observed that a corporation tends to ethically reflect the aggregate of the individual ethics of its top managers. Take a good look at the top managers in your employer. If you conclude that you're working for an organization that is significantly out of sync with your values you can either stay and try to improve things from within or, consider other employment. If you opt for the latter, make sure you are even more cautious about where you choose to work the next time.

In any event though, you may find significant relief just from exploring this topic. Many managers that are living an unsettled existence are simply miserable at work and they are unhappy because the basic level of values they have don't mesh well with the people they work for. If you find this is the case, celebrate the fact that you discovered it and do something about it.

(5) Change your workplace. If you are in upper management, you probably have a reasonable shot at success if you determine this is desirable. That's because you have the latitude to install ethically and spiritually beneficial policies and guidelines, coach people in appropriate conduct and tenor and go the extra mile in bringing people on board that share those same values.

I recently suggested such a process to a CEO who responded with skepticism. "What's in it for me?" he asked with a hint of sarcasm. It took me only a second to respond, "well, what if the folks – mostly under indictment or about to be – at those two major corporations so much in the news last year had applied just a bit more of this standard as opposed to less of it?"

Now, the reality is, hiring people with solid values and a good record in making spiritually sound decisions is no guarantee that things can't go wrong. But it's a lot better than going in the opposite direction and just hoping that you don't have people on staff that are willing to see just how far the concept of special purpose entities can be pressed.

If you happen to find yourself a bit further down the chain of command, affecting this kind of change can be a bit more daunting. As opposed to direct confrontation like, "Hey boss, you're really acting like a crook," you might find that gently hitting the empathy button a few times can evoke some reasonable response from senior management. I found myself in a mid-management slot early in my career and was shocked to learn of a practice that my employer was repeatedly engaged in. After biding my time, one day when senior management was discussing this practice in a backhanded way (no one ever spoke directly about it, validating that they all knew how dishonest it actually was), I chimed in, "Geez guys, I don't know; how would *we* feel if one of our joint-venture partners did that to us without disclosing it?" The room went silent for about 15 seconds that gave me the opportunity to think about where the last copy of my resume was.

As it turned out, I didn't get fired for my somewhat aggressive comment. There were a few people in senior management that were obviously also bothered by this practice but never had the nerve (or foolishness?) to say anything. Over time, those people effected some changes in the practices of that business such that it eventually reflected a standard of "approaching honesty." I ended up getting a good offer from another company down the road a ways. My recommendation for that job? Well, it came from one of the senior managers that had been in the room the day I spoke up. So you never know how staying true to your values is going to pay off.

(6) **Consider other employment**. This should always be the pathway of last resort. People in management tend to be unaware that there are a lot of people whose lives they affect every day of the week. Even though managers are sometimes not the favorite reference at the dinner table, the fact remains that managers keep businesses running and that, in turn, creates employment. That employment results in people being fed and clothed and families are provided healthcare to take care of people in those families that are ill. There is no more crucial responsibility in society. If you are part of the management structure where you work, whether you recognize it or not, you affect a lot of lives. If you leave the possibility exists that those lives might not end up affected in as beneficial ways. Without placing yourself in the posture of a martyr, just remember that function is important to society functioning.

144

If you've tried to effect change and have been unsuccessful to the point where you believe that your core tolerance – your essential self — is really suffering because of the culture where you work, then you have little choice but to make a change. I can share with you that if and when you reach such a point; it is very worthwhile to let those in top management know why you are leaving so long as you do so in a calm, professional manner. The fact is, sometimes the people in the executive suite really don't know that much about what the culture is like just one or two levels below where they toil.

(7) **Recognize your life as a spiritual journey, not a destination**. One of the disadvantages of being a "member" in the exclusive club of management is that we become so goal-oriented that we often lose sight of all of the things that we are missing along the way to the objective. Becoming a happier, feeling less under constant assault, better-grounded and more balanced person is a challenging journey of growth. Even though some people have a natural resistance to the word "spirituality" the reality is that we are all essentially "something" beyond just arms, legs, brain and a torso. Once we mature to the point where we acknowledge that – whether we opt to do so through religious or non-religious practice – our journey begins in earnest.

All too often in our efforts to beat the previous quarterly results we forget all that. In my own life I've learned to deal with the dual challenge – that I have both a corporate and a spiritual / personal existence, and that I need to find the balance so that I can function in my corporate existence without having to sacrifice my growth as a spiritual being.

I've learned to do so by envisioning that I am forever carrying around two very different, yet both essentially crucial, bankbooks. In the first one, I have all of my earthly victories; stock account, bank accounts, 401Ks, options – the works. My other bankbook is where I post and calculate my spiritual balances. Was I compassionate today? Was I kind to someone that needed it or did I rush off and make a few extra dollars? Did I take the time to listen to my son…or was I too busy looking at inventory reports? You get the idea.

I end each day envisioning that, for all I know, it may have been my last one on this earth and that when I wake up next time, I'll be reconciling all of my accounts with whatever "counselor" meets us when we conclude this life. As I envision this scene, which "bankbook" do you imagine that I am reaching for to hand over first?

That concept allows me to retain my balance. Possibly a similar concept will facilitate your ability to find and maintain your own balance as you seek to define and enhance your own peaceful navigation through this life.

Appendix Three
Three - 7 Minute Boardroom Meditations

As noted in Chapter Nine, finding the best meditation practice for you individually can sometimes be challenging. Some people that learn meditation do some initial experimentation and end up with a single technique that makes them completely comfortable and accommodates their objectives for meditation as well. Others, as illustrated through some of the case studies, prefer to mix their techniques or change from one type of practice to another as time passes by. If you follow the instructions provided in Chapter Nine carefully you should have resolved all of those issues to your satisfaction.

Recognizing that as managers you might have a need for intermittent brief meditation methods for those times and venues when there might not be adequate opportunities to engage in a full session, I've summarized four of the most effective practices that can be effected almost anywhere and when your time is likely to be limited.

Having made your way through the practices described in the book, you should not find any of these practices overly complicated or challenging. These particular methods can be inserted whenever it is convenient and without limitation except for those advisories that apply specifically to certain techniques. In those cases, I have provided the specific advisory in the text describing the specific practice.

Essential Cloud Meditation

Most people upon hearing the name of this meditation are tempted to think that it might be limited in practice to days when the weather might be compromised to a degree. In this case though, the "clouds" are only a manner of speaking.

When & Where: This is a great practice if you have five minutes and just need to give your mind a rest. It is not a particularly deep meditation but if practiced with diligence, can be very effective in effecting a solid period of distraction thus affording the mind a true "rest period" during which it can recharge. I perform this meditation waiting in doctor's offices, taking a few moments for myself before an important meeting starts or at the airport when my flight is delayed (usually by a lot more than five minutes!).

Duration: Cloud meditation can be performed for as little as a few minutes to as long as a half hour. While it is true that meditation masters are very proficient at executing cloud meditation for hours on end, until you become extremely proficient in this form of practice I recommend that you limit your cloud practice to 10 minutes or less at a time. Feel free to perform this practice as many times a day as you like, particularly if you are able to attribute benefit to the practice.

Advisories: Since this exercise is most effective if performed with your eyes closed, common sense indicates not to perform this mediation while driving, flying or even guiding a golf cart.

Method: Begin by effecting one minute or so of your Mindfulness of Breath practice. This part of the exercise is merely to create some initial calm. Having slowed you mind down just a bit, begin by observing each thought as it comes into your awareness. The reason that this is called "cloud meditation" is that in the practice, we attempt to "encase" each thought, idea, and notion – really anything that drifts into your thoughts – in an individualized cloud. I liken it to what we see in the comic strips where there is a small "balloon" that encapsulates the dialogue attributed to each character.

The idea in this case is to visualize each idea, thought, concept or whatever drifts into your mind, without judgment or analysis of any kind. You are simply an observer that is watching each cloud come along and pass across the vista in much the same way. Just as you would if you were outdoors and taking note of passing clouds in that venue, you have no vested interest one way or another where a cloud might have originated or where it is going after it leaves your field of view.

What To Watch For: be careful not to allow yourself to be drug "into" any cloud. It is easy to identify with a thought that comes across (oh, here's the damn inventory problem) and begin the internal dialogue in an effort to resolve the issue. Remember, you are an impartial observer in this process. If you find yourself involved in analysis or dialogue relative to one of your clouds, just tell yourself to "release the cloud" and wait for the next one to come along.

You needn't engage in introspection or journaling after you perform this practice. Naturally, you can if you like but the purpose of this practice is merely to increase your awareness of the creations of your mind without becoming judgmental about what arises from it. If you allow yourself to really let go into this practice, you will become completely absorbed in the activity of "watching the clouds" and since your mind is truly resting during that period, you should find yourself energized and clear headed as you come out of the meditation. As you do so, allow yourself a minute or two to regain your bearings.

Walking Meditation

I was never a big fan of walking meditation until I had open heart surgery at 48 and my doctor left little to the imagination about how important it was for me to exercise. It didn't take me long to learn how to integrate basic walking meditation into the other agendas the doctor had so now this has become one of my essential practices. I also have to admit, I've noted several entries in my own meditation journal that clearly indicate a number of beneficial outcomes that trace their way back to when I began this practice.

There's another powerful benefit to this practice. When I was actively involved in running businesses, I was very aware that sometimes, just to enhance my perspective – and maybe to save someone's scalp if I was really agitated – I'd get up, go outside and take a brief walk. If you have the latitude to do this at work I highly recommend that you integrate one walking meditation a day into your overall meditation practice whether you do that at lunchtime or some other time during the day.

When & Where: It may sound a bit odd but I have found that doing walking meditation outdoors is far more beneficial than indoors. I point this out because I know that some people that go to malls in the winter in order to walk for exercise have shared with me that the physical obstacles that they encounter while trying to perform walking meditation inside have become distractions to the practice. Even if you happen to work in a very large corporate office building, I recommend that you not attempt walking meditation within the building proper unless you're trying for an early pension on psychiatric grounds (you'll understand when you get to the methodology portion of this practice).

Duration: Walking meditation can actually be performed for any duration that you are comfortable with. I suggest that when you start out though that you limit your practice to five to ten minute stretches until you are able to execute the practice effortlessly. As noted above, walking meditation can be performed as many times in one day as you'd like but I find it most effective if it is brought into an overall practice regimen no more than once a day or, even inconsistently, just when you feel like taking a walk. The difference being, when you walk now you'll also be meditating.

Advisories: Again, this may sound a bit odd but, please be very careful if you are practicing walking meditation anywhere even vaguely close to where motor vehicles of any kind are in operation. While you clearly do not surrender your consciousness when you perform walking mediation, you do deeply enhance your concentration on the actual process of walking. As a product of that concentration all kinds of potential outcomes are possible, including losing track of where you walked (I note this only because that is precisely what happened the first time I did a walking meditation). Just be careful and, start out slowly until you learn the practice.

Method: Walking meditation is actually an awareness or mindfulness practice. In the process of walking wherever you

153

are going the objective is to become mindful – very mindful in fact – not solely of the fact that you are walking but of each and every facet of the process of walking. If it sounds too simple just wait until you actually try it.

Begin by walking very slowly with your hands at your sides. While it is important to leave your hands at your sides it is also important that they are not held there so rigidly that it detracts from your focus on your walking. Keep your eyes focused straight ahead in front of you and begin to take slow deliberate steps. As you take each step, remind yourself that you are being mindful of the specific activity by articulating exactly what it is you are doing.

When you first begin this practice you may find it a bit frustrating since you need to be mindful of each action you are taking. When I perform walking mediation I actually say to myself, "Foot up, stepping, foot down" and do so for every step that I take. At the outset of learning this practice it must have taken me about 15 minutes to cover 50 feet. What made it worse was that I could hear Dzongsar trying as hard as he could not to laugh himself silly (now you know why I advised you not to practice this in your corporate headquarters building.)

Here are the simple facts though about walking meditation; at first, it is true, you may look like a blind man wearing 100-pound boots making his way through a minefield (Dzongsar's words). But after you practice this a few times you'll establish a slow and deliberate cadence that will facilitate reasonable movement and the core objective of the practice, to deeply enhance mindfulness of a specific activity, in this case, walking.

As I said above, I have found that this is a very valuable adjunct practice particularly in dealing with stressful periods. If you're self conscious, find someplace to practice this technique out of the view of the executive suite.

What To Watch For: Be careful in your objective to effect the practice without looking like you forgot how to walk (some of Dzongsar's good-natured statements about how I looked when I first tried this practice aren't even suitable to share here), not to adopt an Army-like cadence in the practice. It is not a march but a slow, deliberate pacing of sorts. As you practice it you will find that you are able to pick up the pace somewhat without feeling like a drill Sergeant is calling out the steps for you.

What you will find utterly amazing though after you integrate this technique into your repertoire is that you will end up traversing some distance and be completely unaware of the fact that you were walking to do so. As with other meditation techniques, this is the very definition of a successful endeavor since, during that period of "non-awareness" your mind was solidly at rest.

Tree House Meditation

I shuddered when I first heard the name of this practice. It was taught to me not by Dzongsar but someone that I met on the train in New York one way that was a very accomplished practitioner had some interesting techniques that I had never even heard of. When she first shared the name of the meditation I figured it was either the worst line I'd ever heard or that she was just testing me to see what kind of a reaction I might have. As it turns out, this is not only a very effective meditation technique but also a solid "distractive" methodology that can be used to teach anyone, including children, basic meditation methods.

When & Where: This is a perfect practice if you have no more than ten minutes and all you are trying to accomplish is to take your mind away from some other issue that has you distracted. Even though this is not a particularly intensive meditation I have found that it is very effective if someone is unable to focus for the time being on a mediation practice that requires greater concentration.

Duration: Oddly enough this is one of the few meditations that does have a very practical minimum time limit, which I'd place in the neighborhood of seven minutes. It's difficult to envision effecting this practice for much more than 15 minutes at a time and this is not a form of practice that should be integrated into an every day routine. The Tree House practice definitely falls into the "every now and then for amusement and distraction" category.

Advisories: Since this is also an "eyes closed" meditation practice all of the usual admonitions about not driving or otherwise engaging in any activity where having your eyes open would be advisable obviously apply.

Method: The objective in the Tree House practice is simply to apply a very high level of creative concentration in an effort to construct an imaginary tree house within your mind's eye. For any of you that just uttered, "Now that's ridiculous" I suggest that you go off and spend the next ten minutes attempting the exercise and see just how detailed a construction you are able to create.

For the rest of you that might have some trouble getting started in this practice, here are some of the initial visualizations that can aid the mind in the initial sages of construction. What does the tree look like? No matter how silly you think the exercise might be, where would you nail in the first four boards? Why there? Where are you going to put the roof? How are you going to get from the ground into the tree house – if there's going to be a trap door in the floor for entry, did you put the first four boards in the right place?

I am not the most adept person in the world by a long shot with a hammer but, I must admit that for someone that found the very idea of such an exercise being a ridiculous meditation at first blush that I have been working on the same tree house in my mind for several years now. It has several levels and if pressed to do so, I could probably go out to the woods now and build it from what I have constructed in my mind over the years. Many people that dismiss this exercise the fastest end up being the most addicted to the practice as time passes by.

Here's the good news; it doesn't have to be a tree house. It can be a real house, a boat, an island retreat or a base on planet X-71 if that's your thing. What is crucial is the detail and your focus on the interconnection of the various components of your construct. If you're tempted to dismiss this as a viable practice, do yourself a favor; try it once or twice and see just how distracted you end up. Most people that apply themselves with diligence to the exercise are almost always surprised to learn how much time has passed while they have been engaged in the practice.

What To Watch For: If you notice that your mind consistently starts to wander off into completely unrelated areas of thought you have two choices. First, you can simply explore where your mind went in a completely non-judgmental, objective manner. Almost as though you had shifted into cloud meditation.

Another choice is to gently pull your mind back and attempt to create focus on the project at hand. One meditation student told me that he wasn't certain whether he was actually being distracted from the process or just being thorough in it. When I asked him what he meant he told me that in his mind, he would leave the tree house, get in his car and drive down to the hardware store to see if certain items would fit into his design. There's always one apple polisher.

Odd as it may seem, this form of meditation is known to have actually saved one person's life. A prisoner of war that actually survived to tell of his experiences had been held at the infamous "Hanoi Hilton" (a place where unspeakable atrocities and torture were said to be the very reason for its existence). In an effort to compensate for the torture and suffering he endured, in this prisoner's mind he began to construct the home that he envisioned that he would build when he returned home someday. Over the course of several years – literally in between sessions where he was tortured almost to death – he created each an every detail of the house. No doubt, over that period of time he probably could have shared where each nail would be placed.

When that prisoner of war eventually came home in 1973 after taking the more than well-deserved time to try to adjust to his experiences, he set out to build that house. He succeeded not only in building the house precisely as he reported envisioning it but more importantly, he credits his intense focus on that project to that degree of specificity as the single most significant factor in his survival.

This man knew nothing about meditation or, that he was meditating the entire time he was engaged in his little "tree house" practice. I remember that story every time I engage in that practice as a reminder of what we can accomplish if we will only learn to focus.

Remember, never admonish yourself for doing something "wrong" when you are meditating or attempting to meditate.

Never attempt to "control" your thoughts. If it's not a good time for you to practice, don't. In a similar light though, don't ever feel that you are in any way limited by how much meditation you can do. If you have ten minutes and you feel like adding to your tree house – or your dream house – don't feel guilty about giving your mind that break. When you do so, you and everyone that you know benefits.

Good luck!

Also by Charles Graybar

Beyond the Broken Gate

An Ordinary Man's Extraordinary
Experience In Learning Who We Are,
Why We Live And Where We're Going